James Steuart

Notes on Ceylon and Its Affairs

During a Period of Thirty-Eight Years, Ending in 1855

James Steuart

Notes on Ceylon and its Affairs
During a Period of Thirty-Eight Years, Ending in 1855

ISBN/EAN: 9783337230159

Printed in Europe, USA, Canada, Australia, Japan

Cover: Foto ©Suzi / pixelio.de

More available books at **www.hansebooks.com**

NOTES ON CEYLON

AND ITS AFFAIRS,

DURING A PERIOD OF THIRTY-EIGHT YEARS, ENDING IN 1855.

TO WHICH ARE APPENDED

SOME OBSERVATIONS ON THE ANTIQUITY

OF

POINT DE GALLE, AND ON THE PEARL FISHERY.

ı

———————

BY JAMES STEUART,

OF COLPETTY.

———————

LONDON:
PRINTED FOR PRIVATE CIRCULATION.
———
1862.

Some of the Notes on passing events, from which this Volume is compiled, have already appeared in print at Colombo; but as they extend over a period in the history of Ceylon, during which important changes in its system of government have been on trial, their re-appearance, with several others printed for gratuitous circulation in the Island, may not be unacceptable to the inhabitants, although not of sufficient interest for publication.

Worcester, 1862.

Note.—Some repetitions in the first Papers may be objected to; but, as the Governors of Ceylon were so frequently changed, they were unavoidable.

CONTENTS.

PART I.

CHAPTER I.

PART II.

OBSERVATIONS ON SIR JAMES EMERSON TENNENT'S "ACCOUNT OF CEYLON."

PART III.

A BRIEF NOTICE OF THE PEARL FISHERY ON THE COAST OF CEYLON.

PART I.

NOTES ON CEYLON.

NOTES ON CEYLON.

CHAPTER I.

ON referring to the " Chronological table of events connected with Ceylon," in the Ceylon Almanack published at the Government printing-office at Colombo in 1852, it will be seen that it was on the 16th of February, 1796, that the Dutch Government at Colombo surrendered all authority in and over the maritime provinces of the Island of Ceylon to the British forces under Colonel Stuart and Captain Gardner, R.N. ; and that, with the exception of the mountain zone, ruled by the King of Kandy, the Island became subject to the Presidency of Fort St. George, and civil officers were sent from Madras to administer the government.

In the succeeding year, 1797, an attempt was made to levy a tax of one fanam annually (which at that time was equal to about twopence) upon all fruit-bearing trees. As the produce of these trees, particularly that of the cocoanut and the palmyra, formed the chief support of most of the inhabitants, the collection of this direct tax occasioned general dissatisfaction, and led to a revolt, which " finally induced or compelled the Government to abandon the tax altogether." *

---

* Bertolacci, page 33.

B

On the 12th of October, 1798, the Honourable Frederick North arrived from England and relieved the authorities from Madras of the administration. From this period Ceylon became an Indian possession of the Crown, ruled by a Governor *in* Council. Under this form of government, the Governor was individually responsible to the Sovereign and the Imperial Parliament of Great Britain.

It is supposed, that an opinion prevailed in those early days of English rule, that Ceylon might eventually revert to the Dutch. The Roman Dutch law was continued in force, the Dutch currency was retained, and the accounts of the Island kept in rix dollars; the few Dutch Presbyterians who did not leave the Island, remained in undisturbed possession of their religious edifices; and their minister at Colombo—who was about to follow his more wealthy countrymen to Batavia—was induced by Governor North to remain with the remnant of his Colombo flock.* The salary allowed him by the English was subsequently increased to his successors, and is continued to the Dutch Presbyterian Chaplain of the present day. The banqueting hall of the Dutch Government House was appropriated to the celebration of the services of the Church of England, and it is now known as St. Peter's Church. The English Governor contented himself with a house which had been the residence of a Dutch merchant, and a small portion of its walls may be traced in the Queen's House of the present day.

On the 31st of January, 1803, Governor North commenced hostilities against the King of Kandy, whose enmity to the British continued until his death in May, 1805.

The Honourable Frederick North was relieved of his government by Lieut.-General Sir Thomas Maitland, on the 19th July, 1805. The laws and regulations promulgated

---

* This fact was communicated by the son of the Dutch minister who was thus induced to remain.

during Governor Maitland's administration, have been considered remarkable for the soundness of the principles
upon which they are based. This eminent officer left
Ceylon in charge of Major-General Wilson in March, 1811,
and General Brownrigg arrived as Governor in March,
1812.

Soon after this period the cruelties of the Kandian King
were pressed upon the attention of the English by the Chiefs
and the people of that oppressed nation; and in November,
1814, " two native traders from the British territory were
cruelly tortured and mutilated" by order of that horrible
tyrant. Governor Brownrigg, conceiving it to be his duty to
put a stop to these enormities, resolved on obtaining possession
of the Kandian country, and put an end to the anomaly of
Ceylon being called a British possession while such cruelties
were practised by a native tyrant reigning within the circle of
the British territories. On the 10th of January, 1815, His
Excellency nobly incurred the sole responsibility of commencing the Kandian war, in opposition to the advice of every
member of his Council; but, to the credit of all its members,
they afforded him every assistance in their power, and
eventually congratulated him on his success, acknowledged the justice of the war, and the wisdom that planned
it.*

On the 18th of February following, the King of Kandy was
taken prisoner at Gallehewatte, in Doombera; on the 2nd of
March a convention was concluded between Governor Brownrigg and the Kandian Chiefs for deposing the King and
establishing the British Government in the Kándian provinces; and on the 24th of January, 1816, the ex-King of
Kandy and his family embarked in H.M. ship *Cornwallis* for
Madras. In acknowledgment of these important services

---

* These facts were stated by a member of the Council at a banquet
given to Sir Robert Brownrigg previous to his embarkation for England
in February, 1820.

General Brownrigg was created a Baronet of the United Kingdom.

On the 21st of October, 1816, Bishop Middleton—the first Bishop of India—visited Ceylon; preached in the Fort Church at Colombo (that which had been the banqueting-hall of the Dutch Governor's house); formed a district committee of the Society for Promoting Christian Knowledge, and embarked for Calcutta on the 30th. In the course of this year the two first Churches built by the English,—St. Thomas for the Tamils and St. Paul's for the Singhalese,—were opened in Colombo. A Wesleyan Mission Chapel was also completed towards the close of the year.

On the 10th of September, 1817, the Kandians, under the influence of their Priests and the command of their Chiefs, commenced a Rebellion; and within six days Mr. Wilson, the Resident of Ouvah, was killed by the rebels at Welasse. A reward of 1,000 rix dollars was offered for the apprehension of the Pretender; and on the 21st of February, 1818, martial law was proclaimed in the Kandian provinces. At the time this Rebellion commenced the military strength of the Island consisted of H.M. 19th, 73rd, and 83rd regiments of the line, and two companies of the Royal Artillery; the 1st Ceylon regiment of Malays, 2nd Ceylon regiment of Sepoys, a corps of Lascoreens, and one of Pioneers and Gun Lascars. In addition to this considerable force, it was found necessary to call for reinforcements from India, and H.M. 59th foot and a Brigade of Sepoys were obtained from Calcutta, and a detachment of H.M. 86th foot and a Brigade of Sepoys from Madras. The suppression of this Rebellion was not completed until the 2nd of November, 1818. It was attended with the loss of many valuable lives; and the number of European fatherless children was so great as to excite general sympathy, and induce the benevolent Lady Brownrigg to prevail on an elderly medical officer to transfer to the Local Government his right of property in a house and ground at Colpetty to be converted into an Asylum for these poor orphans, on condition that a small Government annuity should be paid him during his life, which has long since ceased.*

From the close of the Rebellion in November, 1818, the whole Island of Ceylon was ruled as an Indian possession of the Crown by a military Governor, assisted in Council by the Chief Justice, the Chief Secretary to Government, the Commissioner of Revenue and the Treasurer; the local administration of the Kandian provinces being entrusted to the officer commanding the troops and two Civil Commissioners: while the officers commanding the several minor military posts, which were necessary in a country so recently subdued, were entrusted with the civil and judicial administration of their respective districts.†

General Sir Robert Brownrigg, Bart., resigned the charge of the Island to Major-General Sir Edward Barnes, K.C.B., who had arrived from England as Lieut.-Governor; and His

---

* Of late years the number of European troops in Ceylon has been greatly reduced, and a corresponding reduction has taken place in the number of orphans in the Asylum. This reduction was, on a recent occasion, made a pretext for removing these poor children to a small house in the Pettah, or native town, in order that their airy and commodious Asylum might be sold in aid of the public revenue. After the premises had been advertised for sale, it was discovered that they could not be legally conveyed to a purchaser, or let for any other purpose than that for which they had been conveyed to the Government; and, on the remonstrance of the highest military authority, these poor children were sent back to their comfortable quarters at Colpetty. Nevertheless, as it has been erroneously represented that the property appropriated to the Asylum was bought on account of the Local Government by Sir Edward Barnes, and appropriated by him to an Orphan Asylum, as it might have been to any other purpose, it is fortunate that the founding of this Institution is within the memory of persons still living; and now that the subject is well understood at the Horse Guards, the orphans of British soldiers dying while on service in Ceylon are not likely to be again deprived of their Asylum. See an article on this subject in the Colombo *Overland Observer* for February, 1857.

† These eight or nine officers were selected from the regiments serving in the Island, and their civil administration gave satisfaction to the Governor and the people, while their judicial proceedings met with unqualified praise from the highest legal authority.

Excellency embarked for England on the 1st of February, 1820. It was then that Sir Edward Barnes commenced his grand military road from Colombo to Kandy, which has been so deservedly praised as the best means of securing the territory acquired by his gallant predecessor. Sir Edward Barnes conciliated all classes of the community; and the members of the Civil Service presented him with a splendid piece of plate on his being relieved by the Honourable Sir Edward Paget, as Governor and Commander-in-Chief, on the 2nd of February, 1822. Lieut.-General Sir Edward Paget—whom to know was to admire—remained less than ten months in Ceylon, when he was ordered to assume the chief command of the armies in Bengal; and until the return of Sir Edward Barnes, who was appointed to succeed him as Governor, the affairs of the Island devolved on Major-General Sir James Campbell, whom Sir Edward Barnes relieved on the 18th of January, 1824.

CHAPTER II.

ON assuming the government, Sir Edward Barnes, with renewed energy, pressed forward the completion of his grand
military road from Colombo to Kandy. The Kandian Chiefs
were astounded at its progress through those forests and over
those mountains which for ages they had considered the bul-
warks of their country; the natives generally were struck
with awe at the power, and with admiration of the skill displayed in its construction: while the whole population were
becoming more and more reconciled to their conquerors.*

Such was the encouraging prospect of permanent tranquil-
lity, that, on the completion of this magnificent road into the
heart of the Island, Sir Edward Barnes was enabled to devote
his great administrative ability to the improvement of the
resources of the country and the happiness of the people, who
to this day reverence his name. † They could not help seeing

---

* A civil engineering critic has called the tunnel on the road from
Kandy towards Kornegalle an "engineering blunder." It is, however,
well known that this tunnel was never intended as a specimen of engineering science, but to impress the Kandians with a full sense of the
irresistible power of their conquerors, who, having made a road over
their mountains, could as readily make one through them.

† When the portrait of the late Sir Edward Barnes was placed in the
Kandy Library, the natives flocked from the provinces to see it. An
old chief, who had been a rebel in 1818, was so struck with the likeness
that he was heard to exclaim—"All the same, come back again! Only
not speak!" When the natives of the interior visit Colombo, they have
been seen to bring flowers and place them at the foot of the statue of
Sir Edward Barnes as symbols of their reverence; and not long since,

a sincere desire for their benefit in all that he attempted for
the improvement of their country, and the development of its
resources. By expensive experiments in the culture of exportable produce at his own personal cost; by persuasion, by
example, and by every means in his power, he devoted his
untiring mind to induce them to improve the cultivation of
coffee, pepper, cardamoms, indigo, tobacco, and all other produce of their Island. He also set them an example in improving the manufacture of cocoanut oil, and in its exportation
to England, whereby he increased the revenue exceedingly.
In all that he did, and in all that he looked to Europeans to
assist him in doing, his fixed desire was to set before the natives examples of successful industry for their emulation.*

It was thus that the government of Ceylon, administered
by a General Officer of established reputation, responsible to
the Crown and the people of England, accomplished all that
could be desired, so far as securing its possession to his Sovereign, and affording satisfaction to the natives, the sojourning English merchants, and the members of the public services,—who all joined in raising a monument in Colombo to
his memory!

Until July, 1825, the Dutch currency continued in use, and
all accounts were kept in rix dollars. These rix dollars were
paid to the soldiers at the arbitrary rate of one shilling and
ninepence each; but the officers drew on their London agents

---

when his son was travelling in Ceylon with a friend, the rentor of a ferry,
on discovering who one of his passengers was, ran and laid the money
which had been paid him at Mr. Barnes' feet, declaring that he could
not receive money from his late Rajah's son, and he was with difficulty
prevailed on to receive payment of the tolls.

* The policy of Sir Edward Barnes in Ceylon appears to have been
similar to that which is now contended for by some reflecting individuals
for the improvement of India generally. They desire that the natives
should be encouraged by the aid of English capital to extend the cultivation of exportable articles, particularly of cotton, rather than that the
cultivation, except as examples, should be undertaken by European
planters.

for their Imperial pay, and sold their bills at the current rate of exchange. In June of that year, officers' bills, payable at ten days after sight, realized as much as sixteen rix dollars per pound sterling, which was at the rate of one shilling and threepence per rix dollar. But in July the community was surprised by a proclamation that all public accounts were in future to be kept in pounds, shillings, and pence ; that English silver and copper coins were to be the currency of the Island ; and that a rix dollar was to be considered as the equivalent of eighteen-pence. This reduction in the rate of the rix dollar from one shilling and ninepence to eighteen-pence was a great boon to the soldiers ; but as this alteration was accompanied by a declaration, that bills drawn on the Lords of the Treasury would henceforth be issued by the Treasurer at the fixed rate of 3 per cent. premium instead of being disposed of by public competition, the officers ceased to be able to realize higher rates for their bills on their London agents, and they had to submit to that loss on the rate of exchange which the Imperial Government imposed on the Treasury of Ceylon by its absurd desire to fix the rate of exchange between the two countries.

It appears by a Return of the Revenue and Expenditure in the Ceylon Almanack for 1855, that, during the last three years of the administration of this Prince of Governors, the revenue was in excess of the ordinary expenditure, and that it continued so for the four first years of that of his successor. The ordinary expenditure did not, however, include the Imperial pay of the army serving in the Island, (indeed some portion of the European force may have been considered as acclimatizing for further service in Bengal ;) but it did include the Island allowances of all the officers.

In the early part of 1829, Sir Edward Barnes directed Captain Dawson, the commanding officer of the Royal Engineers, and the Master Attendant at Colombo, to inspect the several scours, or channels, in the ridge called Adam's Bridge, which obstructs the passage of large vessels between the Gulf

c

of Manaar and the Bay of Bengal; particularly to report on the channels within Manaar and that at Paumban; and to suggest the best means of effecting a navigable communication between the two seas. In the course of this service, from exposure to the sun and the noxious exhalations from the stagnant waters in the old stopped-up channels at Manaar, Captain Dawson contracted a disease which deprived the service of a most excellent officer; to whose memory a monument is erected on the summit of the Kadooganava Pass. In consequence of the decease of this distinguished Royal Engineer, the drawing up of the Report on the Survey of Manaar devolved on the Master Attendant, who, being aware of the impossibility of keeping the mouths of rivers or channels on sandy tideless sea-coasts sufficiently open for the navigation of shipping, was clearly of opinion that the only channel capable of improvement was that at Paumban, on account of the comparative shelter it received from the adjacent isles; but that it would not be practicable even to improve that channel further than to deepen it sufficiently to admit of the safe passage of such vessels as were used in the coasting trade of Ceylon and the Presidency of Madras.*

On the 8th of June, 1830, a meeting was held at Colombo for the purpose of considering the plan of Mr. Taylor for opening a communication between India and England by way of the Red Sea, and also between Colombo and the Presidencies of India.†

On the 13th of October, 1831, pursuant to orders from England, Lieut.-General Sir Edward Barnes left Colombo for Calcutta to become Commander-in-Chief of the Army in India,

---

* See Steuart on the Paumban passage, printed at Colombo, in 1837.

† It appears by the proceedings of this public meeting, that a statement had been submitted to Parliament, in which it was shown that a steam-vessel of 265 tons and 80-horse power had run at the rate of nine miles an hour, while the plan proposed by Mr. Taylor contemplated the employment of a steamer of 120-horse power. Such were the views on steam navigation seriously entertained in India in the year 1830!

as his predecessor in the government of Ceylon, the Honourable Sir Edward Paget, had done in 1822; and he left the Island in charge of Major-General Sir John Wilson until the arrival, on the 23rd, of the Right Honourable Sir Robert Wilmot Horton as Civil Governor and Commander-in-Chief.

Whatever may have been the views of the Government of Great Britain when it obtained possession of the maritime provinces of Ceylon from the Dutch, in 1796, and when it relieved the East India Company of their administration, in 1798, it seems quite clear that at the general peace of Europe, in 1815, the proximity of Ceylon to Hindostan, and its Naval Port at Trincomalee, gave it sufficient political importance to outweigh the greater commercial advantages of the splendid Island of Java, and it was therefore retained, while the latter reverted to the Dutch.

The form of administration introduced by the officers who came from Madras, appears to have been continued, with but little variation, by Governor North and his successors. The Civil Service was formed upon the Madras system, composed of Europeans; but the patronage vested in the Secretary of State for the Colonies. Whatever may have been the defects in this parental form of government, it unquestionably insured the happiness of the native races; and under such Governors as Sir Edward Barnes, it would have insured the development of the commercial resources of the Island, unaccompanied by the evils attendant on the rapid changes which have since taken place.*

---

* Sir Edward Barnes left the Island with a surplus revenue of £73,605, a portion of which was derived from Pearl fisheries, which he personally took much pains to promote. These fisheries furnished his successor with a continued excess of revenue for five years, and induced him to reckon on, and to claim credit for, the continuance of surplus revenue; which claim was readily conceded by the Secretary of State: but this concession was accompanied by directions to contribute in future £24,000 annually from the revenue of Ceylon to its military chest, in order to lessen the

The Commission of Colonial Inquiry, which arrived at Colombo in April, 1829, after completing its labours at the Mauritius, was generally expected to lead to some important changes; and its Report has been said to have had considerable effect in producing those which have since taken place. It is, however, more probable that certain changes had been resolved on before the Commission set foot in Ceylon, and that its labours were chiefly valuable in suggesting the mode in which they should be effected.

It was a very general opinion that the abolition of slavery in the West Indies would be attended with a falling off in the production of coffee, sugar, and sundry other tropical supplies so indispensable to the comfort of the people of England and the support of its revenue. It therefore appears highly probable that these considerations had much weight in Downing-street, and suggested the idea that, by means of free labour obtained from Hindostan, the two Islands, Mauritius and Ceylon, might supply every deficiency occasioned by the abolition of slavery and at the same time augment their resources; and also, that as Ceylon so closely resembled Hindostan in all except its insufficient population, it would afford the opportunity for the safe trial of certain political measures in contemplation for the continent of India.

On the Kandians being subdued and a military road completed into the heart of their country, the administration of the government of Ceylon by a Governor *in* Council must have been one of the easiest in the dominions of the Crown, and therefore could not contribute much to the established

---

drafts on the Imperial Treasury. It was also accompanied by permission to augment the Civil Establishment of the Island. This unexpected increased demand on the revenue of Ceylon to meet its military expenses appears to have been followed by lavish expenditure in order to avoid any *further* claim in favour of the military chest; and when the revenue fell off on the cessation of the Pearl fisheries, the payment of £24,000 a year became a serious burden on the reduced resources of the Island, and frequently a subject of complaint.

reputation of a distinguished General Officer; still less was it calculated to promote the reputation of a Civil Governor, which so very much depends on the favourable opinion of his own resident countrymen,—that opinion being wafted on the wings of the press. The annual embassy from the inoffensive Sultan of the Maldive Islands marked its only political relation with another State. The native inhabitants were happy, poverty being unknown among them;* and the few commercial English sojourners satisfied. The public servants had been restricted, by Sir Robert Brownrigg's regulation of 1813, from engaging in commercial transactions unless permitted to do so by special license from the Governor, and they were held responsible for the faithful discharge of their respective duties. †

---

* In March, 1831, a Friend-in-Need Society was formed in Colombo under the auspices of Bishop Turnor, of Calcutta; but so little necessity existed for this benevolent institution, that a member of the committee exclaimed,—

"Who's in need of a friend, let him show himself here,
For here we all are to see who will appear;
Our Island's so happy, with plenty so blest,
The committee is puzzled to know who's distrest."

† A government, responsible to the Crown and the Parliament of England for all its acts, cannot properly be called despotic; and under such parental administration the natives of Ceylon were as happy as those of the Malabar coast are represented to be at the present day in Mr. Huxham's published reply to the Madras Reform Association, on the 16th February, 1861, in which he declares that a legislative council is not necessary at that Presidency for the natives; nor, judging from his experience in Ceylon, is such an institution desirable for the benefit of sojourning Europeans.

CHAPTER III.

The Administration of Sir Robert Wilmot Horton—Free Press—Abolition of Compulsory Labour—Free-trade in Cinnamon—New Charter of
Justice.

AMONG the changes introduced by the successor of Sir Edward
Barnes, not the least important was the expansion of the
Government Gazette into a newspaper designated the *Colombo
Journal*, and printed at the Government press. In the
columns of this semi-official publication all persons were invited to contribute information and state their opinions, and
very much useful information was thus elicited. In due time
independent newspapers became established, and the Government press restricted to its original purposes.* Under rival
editors all subjects of interest were fully ventilated, and thus,
with the breathings of individual opinion, commenced those
ripples which, with increasing strength, have become the
waves over which Civil Governors expand their sails to the
English popular breeze. But, alas! Governors of Ceylon,
like other public men, do not always repose on beds of roses.

Sir Robert Wilmot Horton had gained experience in Colonial administration as Under Secretary of State for the
Colonies, and had long been a zealous promoter of English

---

* As the Roman Dutch law continued in force in Ceylon, so did the
press remain subject to its mandate, which declared that there should be
but one Government Gazette conducted under the censorship of a member
of the Government. But under the English, this legal restriction on the
Island press had become nearly obsolete. It is, nevertheless, true, that
Sir Robert Wilmot Horton was the first Governor of Ceylon who openly
disregarded the legal fetters on the press, and, by the publication under
his authority of the *Colombo Journal*, in which every man was at liberty to
state his opinion, he is beyond all doubt entitled to be considered the
founder of the complete freedom of the Ceylon press.

emigration, which it may be presumed gave promise of his
being especially qualified for the difficult undertaking of converting an Indian possession into a Colony in furtherance of
his own laudable desire to provide for the redundant population of the United Kingdom. * In addition to these essential
qualifications, his generous disposition and unostentatious
conduct endeared him to all classes under his administration ;
so that if success had been possible, no better selection could
have been made. But to this day we have failed to discover
the best means of reconciling the interests of English adventurers with the happiness of conquered races in a tropical
climate.

In our Colonies, properly so called, the native races have
generally retreated before the civilized sons of Britain, and in
such settlements Civil Governors of administrative ability may
safely be entrusted to preside over their own countrymen in
the land of their adoption, and over their descendants ; for
with the ruler and the ruled there is one common interest—
prosperous progression. All having embarked in the same
boat, the Chief may safely spread forth his sail to the popular
breeze and establish his reputation as a Governor. Even in
the Island of Mauritius, where there are no aboriginal inhabitants, the interest of all is so identical, that its ruler has but
to preserve its possession to the British Crown, and to further
the common interests of the colonists by the importation of
coolies, under proper protection, to cultivate the sugar plantations on which the prosperity of the whole community depends. For such colonies civilians may become popular and
beneficial rulers ; but for our Indian and Mediterranean possessions, which are not strictly colonies, military Governors
are to be preferred. †

---

* See Chap. VIII. on this subject.

† Military officers are accustomed to obey while being trained for the
exercise of command. They have regularly to represent, and perform
the duties of, their superior officers in their absence, and, on being re-

On the 28th of September, 1832, an Order of the King in
Council, abolishing compulsory labour in Ceylon, was proclaimed to the inhabitants. This immense boon to the mass
of the people was altogether unexpected by them. It was not
relief from Rajah-Karia, * or forced labour for the State on
the public roads within their own respective districts, that the
Kandians prized so much,—for that service had been required
of them with much consideration and forbearance ; but it was
their exemption from the services they were bound to render
as feudal vassals to their Priests and Chiefs ; and from that
labour which their own headmen unjustly compelled them to
perform on the false plea of State requirements. There cannot be a doubt that the measure was well calculated to make
the mass of the people loyal subjects of the British Crown ;
but without compensation of any kind, it was as certain to
have a contrary effect on the Priests and Chiefs. †

---

lieved of such duties and responsibilities, they fall back on those of their
own rank as a matter of course. In accordance with ordinary rules, when
the Governorship of a Colony becomes temporarily vacant, the chief authority very properly devolves on the senior military officer; and on the
arrival of a new Governor the said senior military officer delivers over his
civil charge and resumes his military duties. In some peculiar instances
this general rule has been set aside by special provision that the temporary government should be administered by the Colonial Secretary. This
apparent slight of old military officers has rarely been attended with happy
results; for such Civil Lieutenant-Governors, on being relieved of their
superior authority, seldom relinquish it with that grace which insures
cordial co-operation with the new Governors. It would therefore be much
better that the original practice should be continued ; and, if ever de-
parted from for some especial purpose, the relieved Civil Lieutenant-Governor should be otherwise provided for and not be required to resume his
subordinate duties in a Colony where he has exercised the functions of
Governor.—*From a Letter addressed to a Secretary of State.*

  * See Chap. X. on this subject.

  † Within two years the first Adigar, or Kandian Chief, and several
others, were tried for high treason before the Supremo Court, but happily they were acquitted. Notwithstanding the Order in Council abolishing forced labour in Ceylon, and that slavery had been abolished in the
West Indies, slavery of a mild description, confined chiefly to domestic
servants in old families, continued in Ceylon up to December, 1844, when
it was abolished by a legislative ordinance.

On the 10th of July, 1833, the culture and trade in cinnamon were declared free " to all persons whomsoever," and the exportation of the spice was permitted on payment of three shillings per lb. export duty at the port of its shipment.*

On the 31st of August, a new Charter of Justice was proclaimed, and was followed by a division of districts, and the appointment of district courts. †

---

* As the culture and trade in cinnamon had previously been held as a sovereign right received from the Dutch, the policy of the new measure formed matter for considerable discussion.—See some further observations on the subject hereafter.

† Like those which had preceded it, this new Charter of Justice proved so defective as to call for another in the course of a very few years, as appears from the following foot note at page 31 of Steuart's Account of the Pearl Fisheries, printed at Colombo in 1843.—" It has been remarked by high authority, that while the Charters of Justice transmitted from Downing-street to the Colonies in general have worked well and been suited to the inhabitants, those sent to Ceylon, although drawn up with the greatest care and by the most able men, have proved so repeatedly defective, as at length to induce the Secretary of State to leave Ceylon—through its local legislature—to frame a Charter for itself. But even here, with all the local experience we possess, it will be found no easy matter; nor is this to be wondered at, when we reflect that Ceylon is not a Colony planted by Europeans, but a conquered country with a climate inimical to the health of European labourers; the inhabitants of which possess certain laws, usages, privileges and customs, in some measure peculiar to each tribe, and which have been guaranteed to them by treaties ratified by Great Britain. It is therefore in vain to attempt to treat those Indians as British Colonists instead of as a conquered people,—and it is this vain attempt that has occasioned so much inconsistency and difficulty in our rule in Ceylon. We profess to govern for the exclusive good of the natives of the country, and devote our attention almost exclusively to make the culture of the soil profitable to European adventurers. It is supposed by some that Ceylon has been selected to prove the effect of new measures in contemplation for our government in India. Whether this be really the case or not, it is well that such experiments have been tried here; for if such measures were adopted by the Government of India, they would sap the foundation of our Eastern Empire."

ƀ/

CHAPTER IV.

Change in the form of Government—Civil Service declared open to all
Qualified Persons.

On the 1st of October, 1833, the form of Sir Robert Wilmot
Horton's administration was changed from a Governor *in*
Council to that of a Governor *and* Executive Council, with a
Legislative Council, under the presidency of the Governor,
consisting of 15 members, of which those of the Executive
Government formed part; and in which seats were provided
for six unofficial members, to be selected by the Governor from
among the principal landowners and merchants. But so little
did the Ceylonese appreciate the honour of a seat in the
Legislative Council, that they could not be induced to accept
it without payment.

The leading English resident merchants of that day had
previously given their opinion, that their presence in the
Legislative Council was not necessary; that it would always
be to their interest to furnish the Government with the best
commercial information in their power, and that the Government possessed, and always would possess, the best means of
obtaining correct information relative to the state and the
wants of the country from respectable natives, as well as from
its own officers, both European and native. Some English
gentlemen were of opinion that unofficial members, appointed
by the Governor, would not be responsible to any one for
their legislative acts; while their assent to the Governor's
measures would shield His Excellency and his official councillors from that complete responsibility to the Imperial

Government, to which rulers of conquered Indians should always be subject.*

As there were no native gentlemen sufficiently acquainted with the English language, belonging to the agricultural and commercial classes, who were willing to accept the honorary office of Legislator, the Governor, availing himself of the opinion expressed by the leading English merchants—that their presence in Council was not necessary—refrained from acting on, and from publishing, the instructions which directed him to introduce six unofficial members into the Legislative Council. At length the change which had been directed to take place in the form of the Government of Ceylon, was alluded to by the Secretary of State in the British Parliament; and on this fact becoming known in Ceylon, those leading English merchants who had deemed their presence in Council unnecessary, were the first to demand admittance as a right withheld from their class by the Governor. Being thus pressed, His Excellency resorted to the expedient of pensioning his two most useful native interpreters on their full salaries, in order that they might become independent members of the Legislative Council in company with those selected from the English merchants.

Consistently with these great boons conferred upon the Ceylonese people—for which they were by no means prepared —the Civil Service of the Island was thrown open to all classes of qualified persons, and a covenanted Civil Service acknowledged to be incompatible with that perfect freedom which the Imperial Government desired that the inhabitants of Ceylon should enjoy.† It was some time before all the

---

* Even now, this is by no means an uncommon opinion, and notwithstanding the present increased number of European merchants and planters, the Governor at times meets with difficulty in filling up the unofficial seats in the Legislative Council.

† The Civil Service has since become nearly as exclusive as ever, and the patronage divided between the Secretary of State and the Governor of the Island.

English residents could fully realize the vast importance of the changes so suddenly thrust upon the people; but they were not long in perceiving that greater privileges had been conferred upon all persons in Ceylon than were enjoyed by Englishmen in their own land: for while in Ceylon they could peel the cinnamon shrubs in the forests of the Crown *ad libitum*, and dispose of the spice in open competition with that produced in the cultivated plantations both of the Government and of private individuals, it was unlawful in England for the people to peel and dispose of the bark produced on the oaks in the woods and forests of the Crown: and that while in Ceylon it was made unlawful to impress carts for the conveyance of soldiers' baggage when on urgent service, it was lawful in England not only to impress such conveyances for military purposes, but to quarter the soldiers on certain classes of the inhabitants.*

The Right Honourable Sir Robert Wilmot Horton was relieved of the government, by the Right Honourable James Alexander Stewart Mackenzie, on the 7th of November, 1837, and he embarked for Bombay on the 15th, being the first Governor of Ceylon who returned to England by the overland route.

---

* After serious inconvenience had been experienced by having to employ native soldiers to carry ammunition for the 61st Regiment when urgently required to march from Colombo to Kandy, an ordinance was passed which conferred similar powers on the Ceylon Government to those possessed by the Crown in Great Britain in respect to the conveyance of soldiers' baggage.

CHAPTER V.

The Administration of The Right Honourable James Alexander Stewart
Mackenzie.

MR. STEWART MACKENZIE commenced his government with an
insufficient revenue to meet the cost of expensive public works
then in progress, and among them a Steamer building at
Bombay for the Pearl fisheries.*

With the liabilities imposed on the resources of the Island
during the transient prosperity of the Pearl fisheries, which
closed in 1837, and without the power to contract a public
loan, or credit on the Imperial Treasury, Mr. Stewart Mackenzie was under the necessity of reducing the expenditure
upon public works, greatly to the disappointment of those
English planters and merchants who were becoming cla-
morous for roads of communication to their coffee estates.

With a due regard to his position as the representative of
the Crown, Mr. Stewart Mackenzie assumed with becoming
firmness of purpose, which gave general satisfaction, those
portions of the Governor's authority which had not always
been exercised personally by his predecessor, and he evinced
an unflinching desire to promote the best happiness of the
people. But, unfortunately, while on a benevolent visit to
the Veddahs, or wild inhabitants of the internal forests of the

---

* This Steamer was built in opposition to the professional opinion of
the officer for whose use she was professedly intended. The previous
Governor had no doubt been prevailed on to build this expensive vessel
for the Pearl fisheries, under an erroneous impression that they would
yield a continuous yearly revenue; but unhappily they had ceased to be
productive before she was completed. She was not only unsuited for the
purpose intended, but equally so for the general service of the Island.

Island, this exemplary gentleman contracted a severe fever, which so alarmed his friends, that the Secretary of State was induced to remove him to the more congenial climate of the Mediterranean. On the 26th of February, 1841, he laid the foundation stone of the Scotch Presbyterian Church at Colombo; on the 30th of March a farewell dinner was given to His Excellency by the society of Colombo; and, on being relieved by Lieutenant-General Sir Colin Campbell on the 5th of April, he closed his administration, which, although cramped by a deficient revenue, conferred much real benefit on the inhabitants, and he embarked for Bombay on the 7th, on his way to assume the government of the Ionian Islands, to which he had been appointed Lord High Commissioner.

CHAPTER VI.

WITH improved resources, consequent on the economy and prudent management of his predecessor, Sir Colin Campbell commenced his administration under more favourable circumstances. His arrival was closely followed by that of the Chartered Bank of Ceylon, to sow money, as it were, broadcast for the use of those disposed to avail of its abundance. The facilities for raising money afforded by this institution were beyond all precedent in Ceylon, and they were as improvidently availed of as they were recklessly extended. As money became abundant, all other things became dear; the necessaries of life rapidly increased in value; the cost of skilled labour soon doubled, and on coffee Plantations quadrupled. The fame of Ceylon prosperity attracted the attention of European capitalists, and for plantations that had cost hundreds, as many thousands were as freely offered. Many fortunes were made by the fortunate sellers, while those who did not sell estimated their possessions at the extravagant valuations of those who wished to buy them—believed themselves rich—and increased their expenditure accordingly. Those persons on fixed incomes who were unable to share in the abundance of the circulating medium, felt most severely the enormous increase in the prices of the necessaries of life, and some of the aged and infirm who before had kept their heads respectably above poverty, were compelled to avail of the bounty of the Friend-in-Need Society, and thus the utility of that benevolent institution was increased.

Encouraged by the Charter of limited liability conferred on

the Bank of Ceylon, the Agricultural Joint Stock Company, which had been organized during the previous administration for the purpose of enabling the Ceylonese to participate in the profits of coffee planting, applied for similar protection for those of its shareholders whose fortunes were risked for the benefit of their poorer neighbours. But, to the dismay of all, a charter of limited liability for the good of the Ceylonese was deemed incompatible with the principles of Free-trade; while, for the benefit of English traders in money, it had, but a few months previously, *not* been so considered. In consequence of the refusal of a charter of limited liability, this benevolent institution was dissolved. Its dissolution gave rise to the following reflections, which will be found in a foot note at page 30 of Steuart's Account of the Pearl Fisheries, printed at Colombo in 1843 :—" If the policy which prompted the refusal of a charter, limiting the liabilities of the shareholders in the ' Ceylon Agricultural Joint Stock Company' be sound (and we do not question it), how very unsound must be that policy which conferred such chartered privileges upon a company of strangers, who trade as cambists to the full as much in money with England and India, as other commercial establishments trade in it and in general merchandize. This money-trading company is therefore misnamed the Bank of Ceylon. We should not, however, so strongly object to its commercial speculations in money with other countries, though perhaps not the proper transactions for a local bank, if they were conducted with no special advantage over other traders; but it is allowed to issue paper money founded on no *real* security to the public. This paper, moreover, is stamped by the Government free of payment of the stamp duty, whereby the operation of the law of the land is suspended in its favour; and, consequently, its paper money becomes equivalent to a loan *without interest* (if not to a free gift), to the full amount which is thus put into circulation. These privileges and indulgences, as well as the limitation of liabilities, are not enjoyed by other traders. They are such as no man, or body of men, should possess in Ceylon, or can possess without fearful risk, in many respects of baneful consequences to the community : moreover, they are inconsistent with the general policy of its Government, as opposed to *Monopoly*, since 1833.

"In the course of a few years, when Bank notes may be circulated to all parts of the Island, let us suppose a possible, we earnestly hope not a probable, case, that the Bank, like Banks of issue in other countries, should stop payment. It would then be in vain to inquire what security this Government had taken for its people's indemnity before it permitted the issue to them of Bank notes, which it had not sufficient confidence to receive in payment of revenue, or for any other Government service.

"Whatever may be the case in other places (with which we have nothing to do), it is our duty to consider the mischievous effects of a superabundant money circulation (particularly of fictitious paper) upon an insufficent producing population, depressing the value of money in regard to labour and the prices of all articles of produce and colonial manufacture for domestic consumption and use; and leading to over-trading, ruinous speculations, and extreme distress. If we consider those things dispassionately, it is evident that the issue of paper currency should have been rigidly confined to the Government; and, as a greater amount of paper circulation is required for the convenience of the public than is *supposed* by Government to be necessary for its purposes, it could have met the pressing demands of the public by judiciously supplying it, under certain limitations and restrictions, with Treasury notes on the mortgage of real, not speculative, property; charging for the same a moderate rate of interest, the payment of which would have resembled a tax on real property, with the great advantage of its being paid voluntarily by the borrowers of the paper money from the Treasury."

On the 23rd of October, 1843, a branch of the Western Bank of India was established at Colombo, much to the gratification of those planters and merchants who believed that Bank competition would be beneficial to them.* While such were the hopes of European adventurers, the Governor became apprehensive of the power of these rival institutions to combine and occasion à run upon the Treasury to cash the Government notes in circulation. It was thus that this gallant old General—whose distinguished early courage attracted the notice of his Chief, and attached him to the staff of the great Duke of Wellington—as Governor of Ceylon, shrank from the responsibility of continuing the use of Government paper currency without a silver army of reserve in the Treasury vaults sufficient to meet the whole of its circulating medium.

* It was not without cause that some of the European commercial community were dissatisfied with the proceedings of the Bank of Ceylon. It had dispensed with the security of shipping documents and lien on the Policies of Insurance effected on the produce against which the Bills were drawn ; but it did not do so at the same rate of exchange to all applicants; and it was generally from those who could least afford an unfavourable rate that such an unfavourable rate was exacted : hence arose dissatisfaction, and some persons, rather than submit to such offensive distinction, resorted to their former source of credit, where their shipping documents were required as collateral security for their Bills.

CHAPTER VII.

On the Government of Ceylon.

It is said that the government of Ceylon has become one of much difficulty, and that the Governor has admitted that it greatly perplexes him. Now it is but a very short time since it was considered to be one of the easiest governed possessions of the Crown. It has no political relations with other States, except it be with the Sultan of the Maldive Islands. The Ceylonese are a people inclined to be peaceable, and are easily satisfied; and the military establishment is ample to overawe their dissatisfied Priests and Chiefs. In short, it was merely the members of the public service whom the Governor had occasion to keep in order. But now it is said that the Planters and their agents—the Merchants—give much trouble to His Excellency, and that the greatest tact is needful for their management. This is much to be regretted; but it is nothing more than the natural result of class legislation, and of deviation from those sound principles which require every act of the Government to be for the benefit of the mass of the people.

In a country where the inhabitants are composed of several races, whenever one race is more particularly favoured than the others, general dissatisfaction is sure to be the result; for whenever those partial favours are withheld from those who have been taught by repeated indulgence to expect them, such disappointed persons invariably become the most troublesome to their rulers.

It was in 1833 that the Government of Ceylon, by Imperial command, hoisted the standard of a non-trading Government and a free-trading people. It will be well, after the lapse of seven or eight years, to notice how these principles have been,

and are now being, carried out. No sooner were the pe-
cuniary resources of the Island inconveniently reduced by the
precipitate sacrifice of the revenue from cinnamon, which was
supposed to be necessary in order to establish a non-trading
Government, than the rulers of Ceylon necessarily turned their
attention to the most ready means of increasing the revenue,
and *that* even by a departure from those principles for the
establishment of which so much revenue had been given up.
In order to perceive the full import of the non-trading principle which our rulers profess but do not strictly practise, it
should be remembered that it implies a cessation from trade,
commerce, agriculture, and in a word, all those speculations
in which money is expended with a view of profit or gain;
and that all such profitable pursuits should be exclusively left
to the people. But the suspension of public works occasioned
by the want of sufficient revenue to carry them on, and the
apprehension that the punctual payment of official salaries
might become impossible, have been deemed sufficient reasons
for relaxing in some measure the stringency of the principles
on account of which these difficulties have arisen. One public
servant was accordingly converted into a cambist, with a
credit on the Treasury to enable him to cash Bills of Exchange secured by shipping documents; and as neither the
price of the Government store of cinnamon nor the export
duty could be reduced without the permission of the Secretary
of State, payment was received at the Custom-house in East
India Company's currency at the increased value of two
shillings for each rupee, which had cost its importer but one
shilling and tenpence. It will be seen that the profit on the
imported coin was equivalent to a reduction in the cost of
cinnamon on ship-board. All public servants were encouraged
to become speculators in Crown lands; but as this could not
be legally done without the Governor's licence, His Excellency's signature to the documents granting the land was
deemed to be the licence contemplated in the 4th Regulation
of 1813, and to convey permission to the grantees to become

planters, with liberty to ship their produce for sale in the
markets of the world. Many of these public functionaries
saw the impropriety of these proceedings, and hesitated to
avail themselves of the indulgence; and some few, to their
honour, have consistently resisted the temptation: while
others who objected to the principle availed themselves of the
opportunity of benefitting their coffers on finding that their
speculations were not objected to by the Secretary ...

When these public functionaries, many of them holding the
highest offices in the country, became coffee planters, it did
not need much sophistry to convince them that a portion of
the public revenue could not be more advantageously applied
than in making roads to each estates, from the produce of
which they expected a larger return .... ing the
outlay of the public ...

This principle, however ...... to .... positively debarred
from its operation and .... interested in ..... directors of their
own plantations. As soon as these by-roads were ......, all
those planters whose property lay contiguous to them became
loud in their praises of the wisdom that planned these so-called
public roads, when only object was to ..... desired was
that they were made at the public expense. Others planters
were kept in good humour by assurances that it was the intention of Government to make roads in all directions for the
encouragement of agriculture and commerce so long as a
rupee remained at its disposal. It has, however, been found
impossible to fulfil these promises; and, as nothing has a
greater tendency to make men dissatisfied than disappointing
them of their expectations, the planters and their agents have
become troublesome to the Government. But if the non-
trading principle had been strictly adhered to, and no de-
lusive speculations in making by-roads with the revenue raised
by taxes on the whole community had been listened to, instead of having a vast number of partially made roads and
traces opened to places of no political importance, we should
have had a good carriage road to Trincomalee, and others of

national importance, improving the communication from town
to town; the revenue collected from all the people would not
have been expended for the benefit of a few; the planters
would have been taught to depend on their own enterprize in
promoting their private speculations, and we should have had
a race of agriculturists and merchants satisfied with the Government,—which Government could then have been safely
entrusted to any worthy father of a well-regulated family.
We are aware that the opinion herein expressed will not be
generally approved; but we have yet to learn that it is proper
and consistent in a non-trading Government to spend the
public money in making commercial roads with the view of
obtaining increase of revenue; and that if it be so, why it
should not be equally proper to expend the public money in
the cultivation and preparation of cinnamon for the same purpose. Both may be done by a Government, or both by private enterprize; but we are at a loss to conceive why it should
be wrong in a Government to do one, and right to do the
other. Nor is it right in a non-trading Government of an
Indian possession to permit its officers to traffic in land and
speculate in plantations, and in the export and sale of their
produce.* By more gradual proceedings the competition in
the insufficient labour-market would not have been so great as
to raise the cost of forming plantations so extravagantly high
as it has been lately. Instead of public officers, in their
planting capacity, being competitors in the mechanical labour-
market, their public duty should have led them to strive—not
by arbitrary means—to check the exorbitant price of labour
which has so seriously enhanced the cost of public works and
the production of coffee; for unless coffee can be produced in
Ceylon at a cost to insure its successful competition with that
of other countries in the markets of the world, the reaction

---

* Members of the public service have since been restricted from such
pursuits.

consequent on a fall in its price would be most disastrous to the people of this Island. To expect such wholesome restraint in Englishmen, whose sole object in coming to Ceylon is to form coffee plantations without reference to any other consideration than their own immediate prosperity, is to expect that which is not possible. But if such restraining and forbearing qualities are not to be found in men paid expressly to rule over others, and to study to promote their happiness, then it will be not only impossible to reconcile or harmonize the interests of European adventurers with those of the native inhabitants, but it will assuredly lead to very serious embarrassment to the Government, and afford ground for great dissatisfaction and complaint from all classes.

It may be expected of men appointed to govern distant Indian possessions for the brief period of five, or at most seven, years, that they should on their arrival be anxious to accomplish the changes desired by their own countrymen with as little delay as possible. But no such excuse can be advanced for those members of the Civil Service who have gained experience by a long acquaintance with the natives, particularly those who compose the Governor's Councils. It is their duty, by respectful representations, to guard His Excellency against committing himself too hastily to any schemes which are not calculated to benefit all classes of the inhabitants. It is the duty of these Councillors to caution, advise, and assist a newly appointed Governor, and thus to guard him from the perils of class legislation, and that see-saw policy of balancing the advantages conferred upon one class by conferring equally injudicious advantages on another. But when the members of the Civil Service become personally interested in those profitable pursuits which are the sole inducement of their adventurous fellow-countrymen to become sojourners in the land, the interest of Englishmen becomes too powerful to be controlled even by an experienced Governor, and is calculated to lead a new one into serious mistakes. The Governor may well complain of the powerful influence of the planting in-

terost in the Legislative Council, where—notwithstanding the
proportion of official to unofficial members is nine to six—in
the recent session His Excellency had to resort to his casting
vote in order to pass the necessary military estimates.

Very much which now perplexes the Governor would have
been avoided, had the Civil Service been wholly free from
speculations in land. Instead of its being pressed upon the
Surveyor-General's inefficient staff, that strictly correct surveys were of less public importance than that purchasers
should have possession of the land in order that cultivation
might be commenced;—I repeat, that instead of such impa-
tience, had roads been opened to properly surveyed portions
of land before they were offered for sale, such lands, being
thus made accessible, would have commanded their full value
in the market; all erroneous expectations respecting subsequent public expenditure on by-roads would have been
avoided, as well as the vexatious boundary disputes which are
becoming more and more rife every day. Previous to 1833
Crown grants were conferred upon condition that a certain
portion should be cultivated within a given period, or that the
land should revert to the Crown; and when an upset price was
subsequently fixed upon, it was at the very low rate of five
shillings per acre. When land was granted on such easy
terms, disputes respecting boundaries were not contemplated,
and, therefore, in all cases where the Government is interested
in these boundary disputes, the most liberal concessions should
be made to the land-owners, as the errors in the surveys of
the original grants are solely attributable to the Government.
The surveyors are merely the scape-goats. Time was not
afforded for correct surveys, and some grants were made upon
mere estimates of the quantity of acres granted.*

The number of Europears in Ceylon, exclusive of those in
the public service, does not exceed 800; while the native

---

* See a letter at the end of this chapter to the Editor of the *Colombo
Observer.*

population is estimated at 1,500,000—or in the proportion of 1 to about 2,000. Still the ability, capital, enterprize, and energy of the very few insures them the position of the dominant class; but as they all intend to return to Europe as soon as they have sufficiently enriched themselves, they should not be led to expect more from the Government than can be conceded to them without prejudice to the permanent native inhabitants.

The governing branch of the Civil Service and the appellant Court of Judicature should be composed exclusively of Europeans, free from all local ties or family connexions, landed possessions, or commercial interests; and experience has shown, that the same restriction should apply to the office of Queen's Advocate. In the discharge of their respective duties, there should be no room for suspicion that any consideration could induce them to transgress their legitimate bounds. There should be no unpaid magistracy in an Indian possession. The roads from town to town, and from station to station, should be preserved at the public expense for the good of all classes. Commercial roads leading to plantations, and the importation of coolies for agricultural purposes, should be left exclusively to private enterprize. It may be necessary for the Government to satisfy the authorities of Fort St. George, that its emigrant coolies shall receive the same protection as the Ceylonese during their sojourn in Ceylon, and that the payment of their wages shall be equally secured. The assurance of protection will satisfy the Government of India, and the assurance of the payment of agricultural wages in full will insure abundance of labour for all purposes from the opposite coasts. Race or class legislation should be carefully avoided, and every act of the Government should be for the happiness of all classes. English sojourners require no special favours; their success and their happiness depend on fair play to all: and the less Government interferes in their concerns, the more easily will they be ruled and satisfied with their rulers.

F

LAND SURVEYS.

SIRS,—My attention having been called to a letter in your paper of the 13th instant, on the subject of land-surveying in Ceylon, and to your comments on its contents, I venture to offer a few observations for the consideration of those persons who take an interest in such matters.

Beyond all doubt, it would be very desirable that not only this Island, but that all others should be trigonometrically surveyed; but when we consider that the whole of Great Britain has not been so surveyed, and that most important parts have yet to be accomplished, it appears rather too much to expect, that the limited revenue of this Island should be applied to the immediate accomplishment of such an expensive object. We should like to have it done: but as we cannot afford it, we must cultivate without it. To say that un-cultivated lands in the central province cannot be sold until the situations of the required plots are trigonometrically fixed with reference to particular points on a general survey of the country, is too absurd to be seriously entertained. Persons may pretend to hold this view of the case; but it is impossible they can be serious.

What I would propose is this. When a tract of Crown land is applied for, the Government authorities should send special notice to the proprietors, or persons interested in the neighbouring lands, to the effect, that at a certain time the said tract of Crown land would be surveyed, and sold by auction; and such special notices should be sufficient to prevent the Government being answerable for its sale of private lands. The direction and length of every boundary line should be written on the plan attached to the title deeds, and there should be some well-defined permanent landmark upon every survey of Crown land. If situated on the boundary line so much the better; but if not, it should be connected with it, and the direction and distance of such connection also written on the plan. If there should be no such well-defined landmark to be found on the land—a circum-stance which would be of exceedingly rare occurrence—one should be made of permanent material. On all such landmarks a broad arrow, or some other mark, should be deeply cut where it is connected with the survey, and the purchasers of the land should be bound, by a clause in their title deeds, to keep such mark in a proper state of preservation. This simple arrangement would prevent disputes about boundaries, save the lawyers a vast deal of trouble, and land-owners much money. All this may be carried on without reference to a general Trigonometrical Survey, and whenever we become rich enough to pay for one, there will be no difficulty whatever in connecting such estates with it, and in laying them down on the general plan of the country.

In a country like this, with a body of intelligent Civil Servants, the Government would do well to require that every candidate for the charge of a district should understand the simple art of land-surveying, and the sooner it is known to every planter the better.

I am aware that much that I have proposed in this letter is unusual; but the peculiar circumstances of this country render such departure from customs highly necessary. Indeed I am of opinion, that it is desirable that the calculations for ascertaining the number of acres in all Government Grants should be recorded on the plans attached to the title deeds.

Your obedient Servant,

N. B.

15th April, 1854.

CHAPTER VIII.

THE reader of these observations should bear in mind that
Ceylon is situated in the torrid zone, and within 360 miles of
the Equator, and that its climate is generally as inimical to
the health of Europeans as that of other tropical countries.
On the mountains in the interior of the Island the air is comparatively salubrious; but it is far otherwise in the dense
jungles which extend from the mountains to within a very few
miles of the sea coast. In the settlements on the seaboard,
where the soil is sandy and unfavourable for rank vegetation,
it is found that prudent Europeans, whose occupation enables
them to avoid exposure to the sun, preserve their health for
several years; but these exceptional cases in no wise affect the
general objection to lengthened residence in a tropical climate.
The rich verdure produced by frequent showers, so common in
the southern and western provinces, delights the eyes of
travellers, especially of those who have recently left the
parched plains of other parts of India, and raises in their
minds corresponding anticipations with regard to the general
fertility of the soil. Such favourable anticipations are apt to
be increased by visits to the mountain zone, particularly if
extended to the sanitarium at Nuwera-Ellia, which is 6,200
feet above the level of the sea. Persons, while under such
favourable impressions, have been heard to express their
regret that the peasantry of Britain could not be induced to
come to Ceylon to cultivate its uplands with English corn, and
to convert its jungles into orchards of fruit-bearing trees to
rival those of Europe. But the production of English cereals

and English fruit, like the preservation of Englishmen's
health, requires the changes of season with which England is
blessed. It is the change of temperature in the climate of
England which enables its people to endure the extremes of
heat and cold in all climes with such great success; and it is
the change of temperature between Colombo and Nuwera-
Ellia which makes a temporary sojourn at the latter place so
beneficial to the health of those Europeans whose occupation
is in Colombo. The constant mild temperature of Nuwera-
Ellia is most grateful to the feelings and exhilarating to the
spirits after a lengthened residence in the lowlands, and its
similar effect on horses and other animals is also remarkable.
It is possible that the enjoyment of better health may attend
a constant residence on the highlands; but without periodical
changes to the sea coast it is by no means certain that a
greater age would be attained there than would result from a
constant residence in Colombo. European fruit-trees have
been reared at Nuwera-Ellia, but they do not lose their leaves
as in England. The peach does indeed give a poor crop of
fruit of very inferior quality; and the cherry blossoms, but its
fruit never comes to perfection. If it were desirable to produce
such fruit in Ceylon, regardless of expense, it is probable that
better success might attend a tree planted in a box on a carriage and wheeled to Nuwera-Ellia to winter, to Pusilawa to
blossom, and to Colombo to bring forth fruit. Any attempt
to colonize the mountain region of Ceylon would be attended
with considerable sacrifice of life; and the race which might
descend from such colonists would soon degenerate and become unworthy of their progenitors. But after all, what is
there so especially captivating in the Island of Ceylon that the
lives of our poorer countrymen should be trifled with? Some
of them may have difficulty in supporting their families at
home, but there they have a climate suited to their constitu-
tions. If emigration be necessary to relieve England of a
superabundant population, there can be no occasion to send
its people to attempt to colonize tropical regions, while it has

so many colonies in temperate latitudes with soils, products, and seasons similar to its own.

These observations have been called forth by the proceedings of the Ceylon Agricultural Society for 1841, and its application to Government to have mechanics and labourers imported from England at the public expense. Not that such an impolitic, unfeeling proposition is likely to be entertained by our rulers; but in case any unhappy individuals should be induced by specious representations to leave their English homes to provide for their families within the tropics, the sad effects of exposure to the sun on the health of Europeans who have to depend on manual labour for their bread cannot be too widely made known, in order that such persons, when resolved on emigration, may seek settlements in temperate climes more congenial to their health, more suited for colonization, and in consequence to become their adopted country.

NOTE.

The following are extracts selected from the Rev. Dr. Macvicar's paper, read before the Royal Physical Society of Edinburgh, and printed in the Ceylon Almanack for 1854 :—

" Ceylon, when first seen by the voyager who makes it on the south, as is usual, appears on the horizon as a beautiful island. The line of coast, everywhere clothed with umbrageous palm trees, sometimes even overhanging the sea, and affording a grateful shade to the fishermen, who spend the best part of their time when on shore beneath them, is generally level ; but it is pleasingly diversified at intervals by sloping headlands (Dondra Head, Point de Galle, Barbyreen, Caltura, Galkisse, Colombo, Negombo), crowned by Budhist temples, or more usually by forts, either still mounted or in ruins ; with little towns and villages reposing in the neighbouring bays. From the whole coast, also, there may be seen proceeding under sail in the land-breeze of the morning, to spend a day in the offing in pursuit of various species of Scomberidæ, a fleet of the spider-like canoes of the natives, of which I have myself counted a hundred from a single bay, many Dhonies or native traders being left behind them at anchor ; while in one of these bays, (the harbour of Colombo,) at the season when all this marine activity is going on, (December, January, February, March, April,) there may be counted upwards of twenty ships of large tonnage, holding an active commerce with the shore, by burden-boats unloading the manufactures of Britain, France, and America, for the use of the Island, and receiving coffee, cinnamon, and coir (cocoa-nut fibre) in return; their naked crews of swarthy Malabars singing the livelong day at the top of their voices to the pull of the oar. On carrying the eye onward to the landward horizon, it is seen to be bounded by a noble mountain-range between thirty and forty miles distant."

"On landing," at Point de Galle, "and proceeding along the coast" to Colombo, "the observer finds himself usually with water on his landward as well as on his seaward hand, the road lying on a bar, planted with nuts and cocoa-nut trees, between the sea and a system of lagoons, often united by canals made by the Dutch when they possessed the maritime provinces of the Island, so as to give a somewhat extensive system of inland navigation, which is alone practicable for small craft during the S.W. monsoon,—that is, from May till November. In these lagoons the water is usually brackish, and most of them are open to the sea or not, according to the season."

"All around these lagoons," and within a mile or two of the southern seaboard, there are seen "forests of cocoa-nut trees, which yield both the bulk of the food and the materials of the houses of the natives. A few miles inland, however, this valuable Palm is seen only in clumps or topes around hamlets. And further in the interior, everywhere except by the road side, and in the districts where the country has been cleared for growing coffee, rice, or ' small grain,' there is nothing but endless forests and jungle, abounding in foliage, but seldom valuable either for food or timber."

"But without wishing to destroy the *prestige* which exists in favour of Ceylon as a field both for the Naturalist and the Planter, I cannot refrain from stating my own conviction, that its chief interest and value, in comparison with most other tropical islands, will ultimately be found to lie in its history and its geographical position only,—its *history* in ancient times as a safe retreat for Budhistical quietude and civilization, when chased out of the continent of India by a religion of more enthusiasm,—and in modern times its *position*, like that of a watch-tower for all India, with its noble harbour at Trincomalie, its general healthiness, and easily accessible sanatarium at Nuwera-Ellia in the mountains, at an elevation of upwards of 6,000 feet above the sea. This humble view of Ceylon I take from considering its Geological structure, which is such that it can never give anything better on the large scale than a very poor soil, and which holds out no pro-

mise of yielding either Minerals or Metals worth the mining." " The
rock-formation of the whole Island, like that of the mountain ranges
of the Ghauts of Hindostan, to which Ceylon geologically belongs, is
a quartzy micaceous gneiss, very similar to that one meets with in
the most sterile parts of the Highlands of Scotland or of New England. In the north of the Island, indeed, on the sea coast, there
is a limestone containing recent shells and corals; and in the
interior everywhere there are occasionally beds of a highly crystal-
line dolomite."

CHAPTER IX.

Civil Servants interdicted from Planting Speculations—Legislative Council—First Bishop of Colombo—Proposed Channel for Shipping through
the Island of Mannar—Proposed Railroad between Colombo and Kandy
—Close of Sir Colin Campbell's Administration.

On the 1st of February, 1845, the Civil servants were again
interdicted from engaging in agricultural and commercial
pursuits, and on the 14th the Civil Service was re-organized.
By the unrepealed law of 1813, all public servants in
Ceylon were required to make oath that they would not enter
into any trade or commercial transaction unless licensed by
the Governor to do so. But the strong desire of subsequent
rulers to promote the growth of exportable produce led to
large tracts of Crown lands being disposed of to public servants, including some of the Clergy. The Title Deeds, or
grants of such lands, bearing the Governor's signature, were
viewed as equivalent to the licences required by the law of the
land, and as conveying to the possessors full liberty to enter
into land speculations, to cultivate and export produce, and to
attend to all the commercial details which such transactions
involve. These infringements of the regulation of 1813 had
been carried to such an extent as to call for some restriction.
It came very properly tempered with consideration for those
public servants who already possessed land. They were forbidden to extend their possessions, and informed that while
they retained them their seniority would afford no claim to
promotion in the Service.*

---

* There has, however, been no instance of an official planter being
passed over on account of his landed possessions.

G

" In June, 1845, the Malabar, or Tamil, member of the
Legislative Council resigned his seat and his pension, and
became police magistrate at Calpentyn on the usual salary.
This native gentleman was succeeded in the Council by the
Shroff of the Colombo Cutcherry, to whom, on taking his seat,
was granted a pension equal in amount to the emoluments of
the office he vacated. It was not expected that an arrangement, not contemplated by the Governor's instructions, would
have been repeated so long after it had been originally resorted to in 1833. His Excellency's instructions from the
Secretary of State require that the six unofficial members
should be selected from among the chief landed proprietors
and merchants without reference to race or complexion. Even
lawyers, as such, are not included, or they might find the
Council a convenient stepping-stone from the Bar to the
Bench,* or other professional employment, and thus be induced to become honorary legislators. It is said that no
Malabar or Tamil gentleman could be induced to become an
honorary representative of his race in the Legislative Council.
But why should such race representation be insisted on ? If
race representation be admitted as a principle, why is not that
most wealthy and industrious race—the Moormen—represented
in Council as well as the English, the Burghers, the Singhalese and the Malabars ? Would it not be better—without reference to profession, employment, race, or complexion—that
the inhabitants of *the* town of each of the five provinces should
return a representative, Colombo returning two, to make up
the six unofficial members required by the Instructions ? There
might be some qualification as to income or property, to insure
respectability in the representatives ; and the franchise might
be restricted to rate-payers, which would be making one good
use of the Assessment tax. Under such a system the members would either be residents of Colombo or able to reside

---

* Not to the Bench of the Supreme Court, for there are many reasons
why that should be free from all *local* associations, political or domestic.

there during the sessions; the Government would be as well supported as it is now; the acts of the Legislature might then be entertained by the Secretary of State as the desire of the inhabitants; and the anomalous proceeding of pensioning public servants in order to make them independent legislators would be abandoned." *

Ceylon having been constituted by letters patent under the Great Seal an Episcopal See, called the Bishopric of Colombo, on the 26th of April, 1845, and the Right Rev. Dr. James Chapman appointed Bishop thereof, it was on All Saints' day following that His Lordship and family landed at Colombo. Shortly after his arrival the Bishop purchased a house for his own private residence; and subsequently, on the grounds belonging to it, he founded St. Thomas' College, and erected a substantial Church as a chapel for the College, to be used as a cathedral until one should be specially provided for the diocese. † In both these good works—the erection of the Church and the College buildings—he was aided by liberal subscriptions.

It is impossible to over-estimate the importance in a heathen land of the Church of England being represented by its three orders in the ministry; its doctrines and principles inculcated in strict accordance with its Scriptural Liturgy; and its members admonished, encouraged, and supported by its Bishops. It is also important that Governors of Indian possessions should bear in mind that they are the representatives of the British Constitution as well as of its Sovereign head; that it is their duty to uphold the Church of England as well as to govern the people committed to their charge; and that they should also remember that it is their duty as Christian rulers to encourage *all* Christian Missionaries as

---

* From Notes on passing events.

† The whole of this property has been conveyed to the Society for the Propagation of the Gospel in Foreign Parts in trust for the Church of England.

independent auxiliaries of the Episcopal Church in preaching
the Gospel of Christ to all mankind.

About this time a claim was preferred by the East India
Company for payment of the expenses incurred on account of
marine surveys, held by its surveying officers on the coast of
Ceylon, previous to the arrival of the present Governor and
Colonial Secretary.* It appeared from copious correspondence,
that during the administration of Sir Robert Wilmot Horton,
an Assistant Civil Engineer proposed to excavate a navigable
channel for shipping through the Island of Manaar, at the
cost of £20,000; that the scheme had been submitted by the
local government to the Secretary of State, and thence through
the Admiralty to its Hydrographer. This officer—whose duty
embraces that of collecting marine surveys—recommended
that, before so large a sum as £20,000 should be granted for
a purpose so uncertain in its results, a preliminary survey
should be made of the coast of Manaar, and of the approaches
to the proposed channel. Accordingly, the East India Company was requested to direct the surveying branch of its Navy
to perform the work thus recommended, and in September,
1837, a surveying schooner arrived from the Chagos Archi-
pelago, and commenced the survey. On the services of the
Indian Navy being subsequently urgently required at Bombay, the survey of the coast of Madura and the neighbouring shores of Ceylon was continued by the Government of
Madras; but it nowhere appeared that the officers who conducted these surveys had made any special report on the
Island of Manaar, the approaches to the projected channel
through it, nor on the probable success of such undertaking.
Nor did it appear that any of the officers connected with the
Naval and Marine departments of the East India Company,
or of Ceylon, had been aware that the surveys had been undertaken at the special request of the Government of Ceylon.

---

* Sir Colin Campbell and Sir J. Emerson Tennent.

As the expense of these preliminary surveys amounted to fully as much as the estimated cost of the work they were intended to precede, it was not to be expected that Ceylon should bear the whole of their cost, and the claim of the East India Company was settled by the payment of £5,000. At the time the extraordinary proposition to cut a navigable channel for shipping through the Island of Manaar was submitted to the Government of Ceylon, it had in its possession, including the original survey by the Dutch, not less than three surveys of Manaar; and that made in 1829, by the commanding officer of the Royal Engineers and Master Attendant was accompanied by the opinion of the latter officer, that it is not practicable to keep channels navigable for shipping through sandy barriers exposed to the action of the waves on tideless sea-coasts. Thus did the payment of an unnecessary expenditure, incurred at the request of an Administration possessed of a surplus revenue, devolve on a succeeding one with a deficient revenue to meet it.*

In the course of 1846 an engineer, employed by a London Company, completed a trace for a commercial Railway from Colombo to Kandy, and some of the Company's scrip was offered for sale in Ceylon. The period was not favourable for

---

* It is said that as engineers have succeeded in their improvements on the tideless shores of the Mediterranean, there can be no reason why they should fail on the tideless coast of Ceylon; but the two places are not similar. In still water, or in the absence of shifting sand, science and art may succeed, and even on sandy shores the natural working of the elements may to some extent be assisted; but it is different with artificial stone-works on a tideless sea-coast, where the waves are continually breaking on sandy beaches, which extend and recede according to the prevailing wind or monsoon. In such places the erection of stone piers and breakwaters is likely to do more harm than good. At any rate such expensive works should not be commenced by any engineer who has not passed several monsoons in watching their effect, and that of the action of the waves on the shifting sands on which they break. In 1824, a stone pier was extended from the Colombo Custom-house to facilitate the landing and shipping of merchandize. As this work extended, so did the sandy shore of the cove within it, until the place where the cargo-

the speculation, in consequence of the depressed condition of the general community, occasioned by the extravagantly increased prices of the necessaries of life. In July and August public meetings had been held in Colombo, and memorials addressed to the Secretary of State, "praying for relief from certain burdens under which the inhabitants of this colony are at present labouring." Notwithstanding these memorials to be relieved of taxation, another was adopted on the 8th of February following, praying for a Government guarantee to the Ceylon Railway Company! Nothing could show more clearly the preponderating influence of the few sojourning English than this deliberate request to have the already deficient revenue pledged, for *their* convenience, to insure profit to the speculators in the contemplated railway; nor could anything be more convincing of its being high time for the Government and its engineers to abandon fruitless projects for controlling the effect of the seasons and the waves on the tideless shores of the Island, and to concentrate their endeavours towards the completion of speedy land communication between the seat of government and the naval port at Trincomalie for the good of the whole community; and by every means in their power save the people from the risk of a railway speculation in which so very few of them would be interested, and also save

---

boats used to be moored became dry sand, and a temporary wooden jetty had to be extended into the sea. On the said stone pier being removed, the sea gradually resumed its former boundary, and restored the cove which affords shelter to the cargo-boats. Surely this fact should awaken caution in those persons who press so earnestly for a stone breakwater at Point de Galle, lest its effect should be to extend the sandy beach within the bay, and in like proportion lessen the extent of the harbour. But this is no reason why the detached rocks which contract the anchorage should not be removed. Heavy gales of wind do not prevail so near to the equator as the south-western coast of Ceylon is situated. The circular storms of the Bay of Bengal have sometimes extended to the Northern Province; but so far south as Colombo they have not been felt oftener than about once in 17 years, and then they were not sufficiently strong to endanger ships properly equipped with anchors and cables.

future Governments from the vexatious embarrassment which would inevitably attend the establishment of such an *Imperium in imperio* as a railway company in possession of a mortgage on the revenues of the Island.

As the success of our planters mainly depends on their being able to send their produce to market at a cost sufficiently low to compete with that of other countries, it is difficult to understand how this is to be done with a considerable rise in the price of labour; nevertheless the planters are continually urging the Government to increase the expenditure on public works, and to guarantee the shareholders in a proposed railway remunerating interest on their investment. Now, among all the arguments advanced for excluding a railway company from Ceylon, there is not one more cogent than the injurious effect its competition in the labour market would have on the cost of labour. In the hands of Government the execution of public works may be so regulated as not to increase the price of labour. Whereas we have seen planters bid against each other for skilled labour until the price has been quadrupled; and if a railway company were guaranteed a fixed interest on their investment, we should doubtless discover, when too late, that the work now so much desired for lessening the cost of the conveyance of coffee, would be the means of increasing the cost of its cultivation, and our planters be less prepared to compete with those of other places where labour had not been increased in price.

The administration of Sir Colin Campbell was attended with considerable perplexity. His reserve of bullion was viewed by the planters as so much money kept from expenditure in providing roads, which they had every reason to expect to be made to their estates, as such roads had been made at the public expense to plantations belonging to official personages. The reserve in the Treasury was also mistaken by the Secretary of State for a surplus revenue, which required his consideration as to the best mode of its disposal for the benefit of the Island; whereas, in truth, the revenue had

ceased to be sufficient to meet the indispensable expenditure;
the official and the unofficial planting interests had made
common cause in the Legislative Council against military expenditure, and the Governor had been driven to his casting
vote in order to obtain the necessary military supplies; the
diminished portion of the revenue spared for public works was
considerably lessened in its purchasing power over labour and
materials by the great increase in their cost; the clerks in
public offices, and other subordinate employés, complained of
the insufficiency of their salaries; and the general community
prayed for relief from taxation. Still did this gallant old
military Governor pursue his course of duty, and at the close
of his administration was sumptuously entertained at a banquet given to him by "the community of Colombo in the
Council Chamber."

Lieutenant-General Sir Colin Campbell embarked for England on the 19th of April, 1847, and the charge of the
administration devolved on The Honourable Sir James
Emerson Tennent, as Lieutenant-Governor.

CHAPTER X.

Grain Rents—Export Duties—Rajah-Karia.

THERE appears to be a much closer connexion between grain rents, Rajah-Karia and export duties, when viewed as revenue to the State, than is generally taken into consideration. Under the native Kings, the Buddhist temples were supported by grain rents from certain lands held in perpetuity, and by a right to the personal services of the people who resided upon them; while the State was supported by grain rents from all other lands, and the personal services of the people generally; such forced labour being called Rajah-Karia, or State Service. These rights of the State were exercised, subject to the control of the Crown, by the chiefs or headmen of the respective districts. The Crown retained exclusive right to the uncultivated lands—both forest and patna or grass—but the people were permitted to burn off the shrubs and grass from the jungles or chenas, and to sow them with grain on paying over to the Government its usual share of the crops; they were also at liberty to turn their cattle loose to browse and graze on such waste lands, and to cut sticks for making their huts and fences, and to supply themselves with fuel. The collection of cinnamon in the forests constituted another source of Crown revenue. This spice was bartered in exchange for the produce of other countries. The Dutch Government attached so much importance to the revenue obtained from it, that, in order to lessen their dependence on the Kandian King, they formed large plantations near their principal stations on the S.W. coast, and rigidly preserved its growth, collection, and exportation, as a Government revenue, under most severe penalties. Thus did cinnamon contribute to the support of the Govern-

H

ments of both the Kandian and the maritime States or provinces. Both Governments' were also supported by grain rents and Rajah-Karia, and the peoples of both possessed the use of uncultivated lands subject to the regulations of their respective rulers.

Under the native rulers of the maritime provinces, the people planted palms—palmyra and cocoa-nut—on the sandy wastes bordering the sea and the lakes, and their rights to the fruit of the trees they planted were respected, although they had no *legal* right to the land on which they grew. As the sandy wastes near the sea were unfit for grain cultivation, the poor inhabitants subsisted chiefly on the fruit of the palms, and built their huts with their wood, and covered them with their leaves. In process of time, as private rights to this soil came to be understood, no reservation of fruit rent appears to have been thought of by the rulers of the land; but as the produce of the palms became coveted by other peoples, the natives of Hindostan brought rice in exchange for the nuts, and thus did commercial intercourse increase the means of the possessors of untaxed palm lands, and render more apparent the advantages they possessed over grain-taxed landed proprietors. This early advantage has been lessened by the imposition of export duties on the produce of the palms supplied to other peoples, and by import duties on grain received from them in exchange. Thus have the proprietors of fruit-tree lands been brought to contribute to the support of the State, although not in the same proportion as the proprietors of grain-producing lands; but the inhabitants have the advantage of consuming the produce of the former free of State-supporting imposts, while they have not that privilege in respect to the grain they consume.

When the culture, sale, and exportation of cinnamon ceased to be held by Government as Sovereign rights, and were declared free to all persons; in lieu of the revenue thus voluntarily surrendered, a custom's duty was levied on the exportation of the spice. Without such impost the purchasers of the

Government, cinnamon plantations would have been exempt from taxation on their produce, and as the high prices fixed on these lands insured their becoming the property of non-resident capitalists, who could not be reached by any local income-tax, such purchasers would have enjoyed the proceeds of the sale of their spice in Europe without contributing to the support of the government of the country from which they obtained it. Therefore, if the export duty on cinnamon should be wholly given up, the proprietors of these cinnamon plantations would become more highly favoured than any other landed proprietors in the world. Indeed, without export duties on the produce of Ceylon plantations, such exported produce would in no wise conduce to lessen the pressure of taxation on the people of. Ceylon. An acreable land-tax is impracticable, if not impossible; and, therefore, without some other property-tax, export duties are as indispensable to reach absent landed proprietors, as a revenue from grain and salt is to reach the mass of the native population. In England manufacturers and landed proprietors are exempt from the payment of duty on their exports; but they are very properly reached by an income or property-tax. In Ceylon there is no income-tax, and even if there were, it would not reach the most wealthy of its landed proprietors, who reside in Europe; whereas an export duty is a direct levy on the actual quantity of produce shipped off, and it is levied at a time when money is at the command of shippers obtainable on their bills drawn against their shipments. Surely if the produce of Ceylon will not bear a small export duty under such circumstances, it would be better to abandon the cultivation of such produce, and leave the Ceylonese to cultivate their own soil unfettered by those modern laws which contract the free grazing of their cattle. The natives complain of these laws, but they should be taught that the abridgment of their free grazing grounds is more than compensated by their exemption from the Rajah-Karia.

Rajah-Karia, under various names and under various

modifications, exists in all countries and among all peoples.
It is a power inherent in all governments to claim the personal
services of the people in urgent State necessity. It exists in
our own country, for all subjects of Great Britain are bound
to defend the State from foreign aggression; landsmen are
subject to the ballot; seamen to impressment; innkeepers to
lodge soldiers on their march, and possessors of waggons
and carts to convey their baggage; and it has been said that
the Sovereign has declined to accept the resignation of a
Prime Minister. This right of the State, as it existed in
Ceylon, was no doubt much abused by the chiefs and subordinate headmen, and it may have been so by the native
Kings; but surely these abuses might have been corrected
by the English Government, without depriving it altogether
of that right which the government of every other country in
the world possesses over its subjects. Nevertheless, the Government of Ceylon was, in 1833, unconditionally deprived of
the power to claim the services of any one of its subjects for
any purpose or under any pretence whatever; and when the
threatening appearance of insurrection in the Kandian provinces urgently required the presence of the 61st Regiment,
the people availed of the privilege so imprudently conferred
on them, and refused to convey the military baggage and
necessary ammunition, and the latter had to be conveyed by
native soldiers. It is true that a remedy for this particular
inconvenience has since been provided by a local Ordinance;
but is not this Ordinance in itself a lasting record of the reckless proceedings of former authorities? It is even now desired to add another such record, by an Ordinance to compel
all able-bodied men to work six days on the public roads, or
to pay a fine of three shillings to the State. Will not the
Kandian Chiefs and Priests be inclined to impress their people
with the belief that the provisions of the proposed Ordinance
are to enforce English Rajah-Karia? But whether they do so
or not, such an Ordinance is desirable for the good of the
whole community.

CHAPTER XI.

VISCOUNT TORRINGTON arrived at Colombo and assumed the government of the Island on the 29th of May, 1847. On the 12th of June his Lordship was welcomed by the merchants at a grand dinner in the new Hall of Commerce. Sanguine hopes were entertained by them, that, notwithstanding the deficient state of the revenue, the new Governor would devise means for providing a railway to cheapen and expedite the conveyance of coffee from Kandy to Colombo. No time, however, could have proved more inauspicious for the purpose : the sudden news of the alarming monetary crisis in England brought distress and ruin on several of the most hopeful of the planters and merchants, and many of them had cause to regret the eagerness with which they had availed themselves of the tempting facilities offered by the Banks to cash bills of exchange unsecured by shipping documents ; for on these unsecured bills being dishonoured in England they were returned in such numbers as to involve the drawers in bankruptcy and ruin, and to cause the sacrifice of valuable coffee estates and other property for a tithe of their cost but a short time before.

In the midst of these troubles the Government, on the 3rd of December, 1847, issued a Minute in which public officers were invited to afford information respecting the condition of the people and the " welfare and progress of the Colony." In response to this invitation His Excellency was reminded that Ceylon was not suited for Europeans to colonize ; that agri-

cultural labourers could not work exposed to a tropical sun;
that English mechanics could not subsist and educate their
children on the wages of the country, nor withstand the de-
bilitating effects of the climate; that the European merchants
and planters already in the Island did not intend to remain
longer than was necessary to enable them to accumulate the
means of living in their native land; that the native inhabitants were composed of several races, each race retaining its
own ancient customs, usages, and many of its laws, secured by
treaties; that if any people had an especial claim on the Government it was the Ceylonese rather than the immigrant
sojourners; that as the European planters had in many instances been induced to invest their fortunes in land by exaggerated accounts of the capabilities of the soil, the climate,
and the resources of the Island, it was right that every reasonable assistance should be afforded them, provided such
assistance was not at the cost of the Ceylonese, who were in
no respect blameable for the losses and disappointments of the
English residents; that the Ceylonese did not appreciate popular governments like the more civilized sons of Britain, and
until they did so it would be both benevolent and politic to
indulge them with a more parental administration, and refrain
from increasing the power of the unofficial members in the
Legislative Council.

It was also intimated to His Excellency, that the Secretary
of State's attention would not have been " attracted to the
commercial regulations of the Island and its surplus revenue;"
nor would he have " determined on a revision of its system of
taxation, with a view to its re-adjustment to the improved
circumstances of the Island,"* if his Lordship had been

---

* Even had the impressions of the Secretary of State been correct, a
few years of prosperity should not warrant any considerable reduction of
revenue nor increase of yearly expenditure; as the success of such speculations as planting coffee depends on the policy of the Imperial Government in regard to the mode of admission of free labourers to the West

aware that the small surplus revenue in the years 1843, 1844, and 1845 was the result of the prudent administration of Mr. Stewart Mackenzie under the pressure of a deficient revenue, and of the money realized on the sale of Crown lands; that instead of the Island being in a prosperous condition, as supposed, its inhabitants were depressed by the high prices of the necessaries of life occasioned by a superabundant influx of English capital acting upon an insufficient working population, more particularly affecting those classes who were unconnected with the speculations upon which the money had been lavishly expended; that the soil of Ceylon was not so rich as had been represented; that its verdure was attributable to frequent rain rather than to fertility of soil; that sugar plantations had been repeatedly tried without success, and that the successful growth of coffee was confined to some select districts of elevated land in the central provinces.

It was further brought to His Excellency's notice, that the proposed revision of taxation was not, as a whole, by any means practicable; that if the export duties were abandoned to meet the wishes of the planting interest, it would not be possible to levy an acreable land-tax as proposed in their stead; that without export duties on the produce of the soil the lands possessed by Europeans would not contribute to the support of the State; that the proposed direct taxes which were expected to reach the natives by means of licences on shops, dogs, guns, &c., would occasion general dissatisfaction among a people who were known to have revolted with success against a direct impost on their fruit-bearing trees which grew upon land exempt from all other taxation; that it was not expedient to lessen the revenue from salt as the people did not complain of its price;* that they did not complain of the

Indies, and the granting of freehold tenure to land in Hindostan suited for such cultivation, which would afford employment to the natives of India and check their visits to gather the harvest in Ceylon.

* In a letter signed " Nota Bene," printed in the *Colombo Observer*, and in a pamphlet, in 1835, it may be seen, from the special inquiry into

grain rents, as since they had been relieved from Rajah-Karia
these rents formed the only consideration rendered to the State
for the possession of their lands, and were in fact the same as
ground-rents in England; that when the state of the revenue
would admit of reduction in the import duty on grain, it should
be reduced to the rate levied on general imports for the purposes of revenue; that although the free import of grain was
right for the purpose of feeding the poor of England, no such
justifiable causes as existed in England were met with in
Ceylon, and without an import duty on grain and a tax on
salt it would be difficult to reach the mass of the natives by
taxation; that among the many recommendations in favour of
the proposed Road Ordinance, not the least was that its effect
would be felt by all classes, as all able-bodied male adults
were to be required to work six days in each year on the
public roads, or to pay a yearly fine of three shillings to the
State;* that it was a great mistake to apply as sound, with
reference to Ceylon and its people, the same process of reasoning which was sound when applied to Great Britain and its
inhabitants, as in the latter country there was a superabundant population always wanting food and often wanting
work, while in the former there was more work than the
scanty population could do; that in England the working
population mainly depended on the successful competition of
their manufactures and the produce of their mines, with those
of other peoples in the markets of the world; that it was

---

the effect of the salt revenue on the working population of Ceylon, that
the annual consumption of each individual was 13 lbs., while the average
in England and Wales was 9½ lbs.; that the retail price of salt for culinary
purposes in the capital of Ceylon was one halfpenny per lb., and that the
poor natives never thought of complaining of the price.

  * Such a law as the proposed Road Ordinance should have been substituted for forced labour in 1833; but *now* great care must be taken in
bringing it into force, as the chiefs and priests will represent the measure as a return to forced labour, and cause great dissatisfaction among
the people.

therefore wise to cheapen their necessary food to the lowest possible degree, and otherwise assist them consistently with the legitimate interests of other classes of the community, in order to insure their success in their competition with foreigners; that Ceylon had not an abundant population, nor were its inhabitants dependent on the successful sale of manufactures beyond their own shores ; that although the exports of England were relieved from the payment of duty on shipment, their proprietors were subject to the payment of income-tax, and of the two imposts the export duty was beyond measure preferable in Ceylon, and therefore the process of reasoning applied to the people of England had no force when applied to those of Ceylon ; that as the natives of Ceylon had ample employment, and were able to afford payment to the people of Hindostan for supplying them with rice and curry stuff, and the Maldivians for supplying them with cured fish, it was much better that such commerce should continue for the greater benefit of all these peoples, each following those pursuits which were best suited to themselves and their respective countries, rather than that the revenue of Ceylon should be risked in the repair of old tanks and embankments in those parts of the Island where such ruins testify to their abandonment by the people ;* that those persons who advo-

---

* Has it been satisfactorily ascertained that some of these ruined tanks and embankments were ever better than splendid failures? Is not the present decay of *all* sufficient proof that even those of successful construction have long since ceased to be required by the people? If the cultivation of grain in Ceylon has become a profitable speculation, how is it that the natives, like the Europeans, prefer to cultivate produce for exportation, and to pay the people of Hindostan to supply them with rice? Is it likely that rice produced by such an expensive outlay on the means of irrigation would be sold cheaper in the markets of Colombo and Kandy than that which is imported from India? Why should the repair of these ruins, at the cost of the revenue, be a more fitting speculation for the Government than for private enterprize? When the state of the revenue becomes sufficiently buoyant to admit of the risk of such great expenditure, would it not be better to lower the import duty on grain to the rate fixed on other imports for purely revenue purposes, and thus

I

cated such expenditure for the irrigation of desolate places in order to induce the natives of Hindostan to settle in Ceylon, should remember that it is the duty of the legitimate rulers of Hindostan to find employment for their working people; and while the working people of Ceylon have ample employment, all speculations for the purpose of increasing the production of grain, like those for the production of coffee, should be left to private adventurers; that it was enough that all immigrants should have the benefit of the laws of the Island, and be treated in every respect like the Ceylonese, whether they came to grow coffee or grain, or for any other legitimate occupation; that it was the people of Ceylon who should be cared for rather than the spot of earth on which they dwelt, which should always be of subordinate consideration to the happiness of the people; that those English planters who had estates in good localities, and sufficient means to tide over the existing monetary difficulty, would eventually be amply repaid; but that those who had been unfortunate in the selection of their land, and those who had exhausted their capital, and more particularly those who had been induced by misrepresentation to leave their native land to become planters were entitled to every consideration and assistance which it might be in the power of the Government to afford, consistently with its duty towards the Ceylonese; and that that which concerned every class of the community and demanded serious consideration was the great public loss sustained by the Company's rupee, which contained only 165 grains of silver, being current as two shillings, which contained 177 grains; that the close proximity of Ceylon to Hindostan, and the considerable commercial intercourse between them, rendered it imperative that

---

cheapen the cost of food to the people, among whom is a considerable class requiring such relief? It may be true, that such a proceeding would not be attended with such *éclat*, nor afford the gratification too frequently derived from the receipt of large revenue, and the still further gratification of spending it; but would it not be better for the Ceylonese?

their currency should be the same; whereas, by the arbitrary value given in Ceylon to 165 grains of silver, which were procured by the Banks from Bombay at the cost of 1*s.* 10*d.* and paid over their Colombo counters as two shillings, the community sustained a loss of twelve grains of silver in each rupee, which was gained by the importers of rupees, minus the small cost of their conveyance by sea." Such were the opinions founded upon thirty years' experience of Ceylon and the Ceylonese, which were called forth by the Governor's Minute of December, 1847. But unfortunately they were not in accordance with the instructions which His Excellency had received from the Secretary of State—instructions founded on representations from Ceylon of a previous date to his Lordship's appointment as Governor—setting forth the urgent necessity of increasing the revenue by means of an acreable land-tax and direct impost on shops, dogs, guns, &c., in order that the planting interest might be relieved of the 2½ per cent. export duty which existed on the produce of the soil when they purchased their estates of the Crown. No time could have been more inopportune for the imposition of direct taxes on the Ceylonese, who had successfully resisted their imposition in 1797. The Kandian Priests and Chiefs, being adepts in the art of dissembling in their intercourse with Europeans, had so well concealed their dissatisfaction at the loss of the compulsory services of their vassals, that many persons, particularly those fresh from England, doubted its existence. But the impolitic attempt to impose direct taxes on the people afforded the disaffected Chiefs and Priests the opportunity they so much desired, and their exaggerated representations of the amount and objectionable nature of the new imposts, added the vivifying spark to the smouldering embers of revolt. The effect was electrical. The Kandians rose in open rebellion, and on the 20th of July, 1848, proclaimed a Pretender to the Kandian throne.

In justice to Lord Torrington, he should not be held in any degree responsible for the causes which led to this rebellion.

His Lordship had done no more than obey the orders of the
Secretary of State to enforce certain measures which had been
approved by a Committee in London, and made lawful by the
unanimous vote of the official members of the Legislative
Council, who are responsible to the Crown, and of the unofficial members who are responsible to no one. In a word,
his Lordship's responsibility in regard to the rebellion did
not commence before it, but with it! It was his energetic
promptitude in obtaining troops from Madras to relieve those
in garrison at Trincomalie, and enable them to march on
Dambool and surprise the enemy in rear, which so paralysed
the efforts of the rebels and astounded the whole Kandian
community; and which—together with the proclamation of
martial law in the rebellious provinces, the gallantry displayed
by the small military force stationed within them, and the
sound judgment of their commander—nipped the rebellion
almost in the bud, and saved the coffee harvest from destruction, and many of those persons interested in the crops from
bankruptcy and ruin. The despondency thus occasioned in the
disaffected Kandians was increased by the celerity with which
the Pretender and other convicted rebels were transported to
Malacca. Thus did Lord Torrington suppress the rebellion
which at one time caused such great consternation in Colombo, and the rapidity with which it was effected crushed
the last hope of success in the most sanguine of its promoters.

On the 10th of October, after the capture of the Pretender
—who subsequently acknowledged his offence—martial law
was abolished by proclamation, and order was perfectly restored. But the check given to commercial and planting
enterprise, by the stoppage of remittances from England,
threw many young Englishmen out of employment; and on
the 15th of October forty-seven of these disappointed adventurous spirits embarked for Australia to try their fortunes in
that more congenial climate.

The Governor lost no time in rescinding the objectionable
taxes, but, as the export duties had been abolished, the

planters obtained that boon to the entire loss of the revenue, and that at a time when the State was in urgent need of money to meet the expenses attending the suppression of the rebellion.* As the Banks had been permitted to exercise the sovereign right of issuing paper currency, the extraordinary expenses which the ordinary revenue was unequal to defray, could not be met by an increased issue of Treasury notes ; and, as under general instructions debentures bearing interest could not be issued, the Government in this dilemma had to obtain temporary assistance from one of the Banks, and the interest paid on this loan remains a lasting record in the accounts of the Island of the error committed when the sovereign right of issuing paper money ceased to be rigidly confined to the State, notwithstanding the said debt has been liquidated.

Considering the frequent alarms since 1833, occasioned by the continued desire of the Kandian Chiefs and the Priests to stir up rebellion, the actual outbreak having been so successfully subdued, and the spirit of rebellion so completely crushed, the occurrence may be viewed as fortunate in its results, beneficial to all classes, and calculated to insure the loyalty of the rising generation. There is, however, one circumstance which detracts from that general satisfaction which otherwise would have attended the restoration of order. At the time when the full extent of the revolt and its causes were not fully understood, an assembly of Buddhist Priests in a maritime province complained of the proposed Road Ordinance which required them to do work which, as *Priests*, they could not perform, or pay a fine which, as *paupers* living on alms, they had not money to defray.† In an unhappy moment they were assured that they should be exempted from the operations of the proposed law. This promise was faithfully kept, and by such special exemption in a legislative

---

* See Steuart's Letter on the Rebellion.

† The revenue from Temple Lands not being taken into consideration

enactment, the Buddhist religion has obtained a status which it did not previously possess. The effect of this unfortunate concession cannot be too soon amended by the legal exemption of all ministers of religion from the operation of the Road Ordinance, without special mention of any particular sect.

The merchants and planters were joined by many respectable Ceylonese in their expression of gratitude to Lord Torrington, for his prompt suppression of the rebellion and the security thus obtained for their property. But there were some—happily but very few—who complained of the proceedings by which such security had been obtained, and, strange as it may appear, these were the same who were so panic-stricken when the news reached Colombo of a Pretender having been crowned at Dambool, as to propose that troops should be despatched in private carriages, and even to speak of concessions being made to the rebels in order to save their plantations from destruction. These ungrateful persons availed themselves of an unexplained sentence in a Despatch, addressed by Lord Torrington to the Secretary of State,* and obtained through their misinformed friends in England a parliamentary inquiry into the conduct of the local government. Encouraged by this unexpected success, that portion of the local press which was under their influence became so violent in its denunciations, that it called forth a counter declaration, signed by the most respectable merchants and other inhabitants of Colombo,† and compelled even those, who had till then

---

* It was reported in this Despatch that the Priest convicted of having crowned the Pretender was executed in his full robes This unfortunate expression was attended with much misconception in England, where it was not generally known that the invariable dress of a Buddhist Priest is a piece of yellow cotton cloth wrapped round his person—yellow being the distinguishing colour of the priestly office.

† A DECLARATION.

We have much pleasure in giving publicity to the following declaration, which has been drawn up by several gentlemen of this community in support of TRUTH and JUSTICE respecting the recent troubles of Ceylon-believed defence unnecessary, to expose the falsity of the charges preferred against Lord Torrington and his Government.

His Lordship having been compelled to accept temporary assistance from the Bank in order to meet the extraordinary expenditure on the means employed to suppress the rebellion, lost no time in commencing its repayment.

Lord Torrington announced the resignation of his office in July, 1850, and on the 18th of October left the Island in charge of the Honourable C. J. MacCarthy, and returned to England with his family.

And as we are sure there are many gentlemen, both European and Ceylonese, in this Island, who would desire to support the opinions therein expressed by their signatures, we should be happy if this may afford them the opportunity of testifying their opinions on a subject which, locally, has been hitherto almost entirely confined to Newspaper discussion.

                                    " *Colombo,* 30*th May,* 1849.

"We, the undersigned inhabitants of Ceylon, viewing with regret the undeserved censure heaped upon the Governor of this Island by certain portions of the press of England, India, and Colombo, as well as with concern the general misconception of His Excellency's acts in suppressing the rebellion, feel it to be incumbent on us *in support of* TRUTH and JUSTICE, to come forward and declare, that the commercial and agricultural embarrassments of Ceylon are not attributable to Lord Torrington, nor to any of his Lordship's own measures ; but rather to the resources of the Island, particularly of its soil, having been over-rated by former Governments and by individuals ; to over production of coffee, and to Imperial legislation. And further, that the late disturbance in the Kandian Districts is attributable to the long-cherished desire of the Priests and Headmen for a resumption of that power which they possessed previous to 1833, but whose hopes were frustrated by the generally happy condition of the Kandians, under the mild and equitable rule of England, until they became dissatisfied with certain Fiscal impositions, which the Governor had been authorized to carry out, as a part of the general Commercial and Fiscal policy founded by Earl Grey, upon the recommendation of a Committee appointed by his Lordship to report on representations from Ceylon respecting its financial condition. We are, moreover, of opinion, that Lord Torrington is entitled to the gratitude of the people of Ceylon, for his promptitude in restoring peace and order in the Kandian Province."—*Colombo Examiner, June* 2*nd,* 1849.

CHAPTER XII.

Cinnamon Revenue.

In Ceylon, where there is such a vast extent of primeval forests, jungle, and other uncultivated land, and where the produce of that which is cultivated is so varied in kind, quality, and quantity, it seems surprising that any person acquainted with the Island and its people should have proposed to establish an acreable land-tax; but how it was intended to extend its action to cinnamon peeled *ad libitum* in the uncultivated woods and forests of the Crown, and sold by the peelers to exporting merchants who were to pay no export duty, is altogether incomprehensible.

It has pleased the Almighty to bless certain parts of Ceylon with the indigenous production of cinnamon of the very finest quality; and its culture and trade had been reserved from the earliest period by succeeding Governments as a source of revenue, which rendered their expenditure less dependent on the amount of taxes collected from the people. In the year 1832 a proposal, which had been made by the Commissioners of Colonial Inquiry, that the Government should dispose of its cinnamon plantations and abandon with its culture all trade in the spice, led to considerable discussion in the *Colombo Journal;* and the letters and articles have subsequently been collected and printed in a volume which now forms an important record in the Island.

After the lapse of sixteen years it may not be unprofitable to reconsider the opinions of three of the most prominent writers on the subject, who were known at the time as " Journalist," " Liber," and " Nota Bene."

The writings of " Journalist" display such acquaintance

with the principles of political economy as applicable to England and its inhabitants, as to stamp them beyond all question as those of a late distinguished individual much esteemed by the people. "Liber" is known to have been a gentleman of much local knowledge, and considerable ability. While these two contended for victory, the opinions of "Nota Bene" were too feebly expressed to command general attention; but they met with some heed from the two contending parties, particularly from "Journalist."

It will be seen that "Journalist" advocated the retention of the exclusive right of the Government to the growth and sale of cinnamon within the Island, but not of its exportation. He would have permitted landowners to cultivate the spice, but would have compelled them to deliver their produce to Government at fixed remunerating prices; and he approved of periodical sales by auction of cinnamon embaled ready for shipping to exporting merchants, and the abandonment of its export by Government. He was of opinion that cinnamon was a luxury that did not admit of much increased consumption, and that no advantage would be gained by extended cultivation and consequent reduction in its price. He denied that the system continued by the Government of retaining the exclusive cinnamon trade within the Island deserved the odium which attaches to monopoly; and he ably drew the distinction between a monopoly made by man and a special benefit conferred by nature on a country and its people, which he designated a natural monopoly. "Liber," on the contrary, contended that the Government of Ceylon in its cinnamon transactions was a great mercantile company, enjoying a monopoly from which all other merchants were excluded, similar to the monopoly of the East India Company when it had the exclusive trade with India and China. He accordingly advocated the immediate abandonment of it, and that the culture and trade in cinnamon should be thrown open to private enterprize; but as the State could not dispense with the revenue it derived from cinnamon, he recommended that an export duty of three shillings per lb. should be levied on the spice. In his first letter he declares that " the trade in cinnamon" being confined to the Government " is a monopoly bearing injuriously on Ceylon in two ways,—1st, positively, in so far as it is productive of actual inconvenience and injury to the landowner; 2nd, negatively, in so far as it deprives the country of advantages which it would otherwise reap from capitalists desirous of engaging in this tempting trade, who would settle in Ceylon."

It will also be seen that " Journalist" and " Liber" agreed that the Government should not continue the exportation of cinnamon; and this was also the opinion of " Nota Bene," who agreed with " Journalist" that it should dispose of the spice embaled for shipment at periodical sales by auction, and *this* was in truth all the change desired by the resident English merchants of that day. All three writers admitted that the law which forbade landowners to destroy or turn to profitable account the cinnamon which grew naturally on their own lands should be amended. " Journalist" would have wished them to cultivate the spice and dispose of it to Government at fixed remunerating rates. " Nota Bene" would have given them the option of doing so, or of rooting up the plants as they would some noxious weed; and " Liber" was for perfect freedom to all persons in the culture and trade of the spice, and thus relieve the landowners of what he called a " positive injury." " Nota Bene" further pointed out that the cinnamon plant could not spring up in paddy fields, submerged as they generally were; that its growing on uncultivated land injured no one, and that therefore the restriction objected to had not been such a positive injury as to occasion complaint; nor was it of a nature not to have been remedied by Government if it had been complained of. He also submitted, that although the retention of the culture and trade in cinnamon might be viewed by people of other countries as a monopoly from which they were excluded, still the inhabitants of Ceylon could not justly say that they were excluded,—

because they all shared in the profits derived from the culture and sale of the spice, inasmuch as such profits were applied as revenue to defray the expenses of the Government, which expenses would otherwise have to be wholly borne by themselves.

Differences of opinion also existed in regard to what would be the ultimate effect of increased production, and consequent reduction in price. "Liber" contended that cinnamon would be subject to the same principles of political economy as regulated the demand and supply of other products. "Journalist" maintained that the consumption of cinnamon would not increase in proportion to reduction in its price; that the number of its consumers would not be greater, nor would those consumers use more of the spice if it cost less money; and moreover that Ceylon, with its peculiar soil and climate, had nothing to fear from the competition of cinnamon-growers in Java and on the Malabar Coast. But "Nota Bene" believed that the consumption of cinnamon would increase with a reduction of price, although not to the extent anticipated by "Liber;" that such a difference between the cost of production in Ceylon and the selling price in Europe as would warrant an export duty of three shillings per lb., would prove too great a temptation to be resisted by residents in Java and on the Malabar Coast; that although they might not produce spice equal in quality to that of Ceylon, still their inferior cinnamon being forced on the market would have an injurious effect on the Ceylon trade; that therefore the growth and sale of cinnamon in Ceylon should be retained and the cultivation extended by the Government until, by increased production, the profits on its sale should be reduced to a scale that would deter the inhabitants of other countries from planting it; and when these profits became reduced to those which were common on the culture and sale of other productions, then would be the proper time to sell the Government plantations and to throw open the culture and trade to private enterprize. But Imperial authority decreed, contrary to the wishes of the Go-

vernor, that the culture of, and the trade in, cinnamon should
be at once thrown open "to all persons whomsoever,"
subject to an export duty of three shillings per lb., with full
liberty to peel the spice in the woods and forests of the Crown,
and that the preserved cinnamon plantations should be sold to
the highest bidders. The Government preserved cinnamon
plantations were accordingly disposed of, and, of course, for
such prices as an export duty of three shillings per lb. on their
produce and the competition which such produce would meet
with in the market from that spice which had been freely obtained from the woods and forests of the Crown, might have
been expected to admit of, and the purchase-money was
expended as part of the yearly revenue.

In tracing how far the opinions of these several writers have
been verified, it will be seen that the efforts made on the Malabar Coast and in Java to cultivate cinnamon have as yet
failed to produce spice much, if at all, superior to the third
quality cut in the wild forests of Ceylon. It is, therefore,
clear that Ceylon is peculiarly favoured with the indigenous
production of cinnamon of the *finest* quality; but it is equally
true that the efforts made in other countries have produced
spice which has contributed to the reduction in the selling
price of that peeled in Ceylon; and that it has been found
necessary to reduce the export duty from three shillings, step
by step, until it has reached the low rate of fourpence per lb.,
below which it is much to be desired that it should not be reduced until the selling price in Europe approximates as nearly
to the cost of production as generally exists between the selling prices and the cost of other Ceylon produce; the time will
then have arrived to treat cinnamon in all respects as other
produce is treated.

It was too much the practice in those days, when
"Journalist" and "Liber" were discussing the cinnamon
question, to represent Ceylon as the finest country, possessing
the best climate in the world; it may, therefore, be seen how
it was that "Liber" entertained the mistaken belief that if

the Government abandoned the culture of, and trade in, cinnamon, its plantations would become the property of "capitalists who would settle in Ceylon." Nearly all the said plantations have become the property of English capitalists; but, unfortunately for "Liber's" prediction, they have not settled in Ceylon. They prefer, like sensible men, to enjoy in England the *revenue* which they derive from their cinnamon plantations; and be it remembered, that the revenue which they now enjoy is that revenue which, under the original system, passed into the Treasury of Ceylon, and rendered taxation less onerous on the inhabitants. In 1832, the revenue derived by the Government of Ceylon from the culture and sale of cinnamon amounted to £90,000. It obtains now, after a lapse of 16 years, only £13,967, and that is derived from export duty. It is, therefore, clear that the difference, £76,033, has to be made up by taxes on the Ceylonese, and that without the least countervailing advantage; for the cultivation of cinnamon is not, nor ever was, necessary to afford employment to the people. They have always had more work than they could do, and have in all ages employed coolies from India. Under the original system, the cinnamon peelers were paid for their labour by the superintendents of the Government plantations; and under the present system they are paid by the agents of the absent proprietors of the same plantations. Under the original system, the profits derived from the culture and sale of the spice were expended on public works, or otherwise in the interest of the whole Ceylon community; and under the present system, such profits are expended by the absent proprietors in Europe, who, with the exception of the export duty, do not contribute towards the support of the Government of the country from whence they derive their incomes.

As an opinion prevailed that great hardship had been inflicted on the Chalia caste, by their exclusive employment by Government in the cultivation of cinnamon, it may be as well to mention here, that so far from this being considered a hardship by the Chalias themselves, when the Government abandoned the cultivation, they actually petitioned to be allowed to retain the privilege they had so long enjoyed of the exclusive cultivation of the spice.

CHAPTER XIII.

Arrival of Sir George Anderson—His previous Public Service—Municipality Declined by the Inhabitants of Colombo—The Political Economy
of England and Ceylon Contrasted—Governor's Economy in Public
Expenditure—Observations on the State of Ceylon and the Policy pur-
sued by its Government—Civil Service, both European and Native—
Supreme Court—Waste Land on the Sea Coast.

WHEN Sir George Anderson received the notification of his
appointment to the Government of Ceylon, it was so near to
that period of the year when hurricanes are expected to prevail in the vicinity of the Mauritius, that he prudently availed
himself of the departure of the ship *Buckinghamshire* from Port
Louis to proceed in her to Colombo, and he arrived with his
family on the 7th of November, 1850; but as his Commission
did not reach Ceylon until three weeks afterwards, he did not
assume the Government until the 27th.

His Excellency had established his reputation in the
Bombay Civil Service, and in the administration of the affairs
of that Presidency as Lieutenant-Governor. On being relieved
of that important government, he retired into private life, in
accordance with the practice of the Indian Civil Service. He
was, however, subsequently appointed by the Crown to rule
over the Island of Mauritius; and in the government of that
Crown Colony he gave as great satisfaction as he had done
previously in the administration of that of an Indian Presidency. Having gained experience in both, he was the more
likely to harmonize the two, if possible, in the administration
of the affairs of Ceylon. His administrative ability had been
satisfactorily tested, and he was not one of those public men
alluded to in the House of Commons by an eminent statesman
when he said, that men of sufficiently high standing in

England declined to become Governors of Colonies unless they were in embarrassed circumstances.*

Sir George Anderson had gratified the people of the Mauritius by conferring a municipality on the Town of Port Louis; and soon after his arrival in Ceylon, His Excellency proposed to confer a similar corporation on the City of Colombo: but, to his surprise, so little did the citizens appreciate popular institutions and self-government, that no one could be prevailed on to accept honorary municipal office, notwithstanding unofficial seats in the Legislative Council had been open to them for the long period of seventeen years. The longer Ceylon is known, and the better the Ceylonese are understood, the more apparent will it become that principles, admitted to be sound in their application to Colonies properly so called, are not always so when applied to Indian possessions.

The proximity of Ceylon to Hindostan, and the general intercourse which has always subsisted between their inhabitants, has produced considerable similitude; and there can be no doubt that it would be greatly to the benefit of the Ceylonese if their currency were the same as that of Hindostan.† Nevertheless, there are some important differences between the Presidencies and their neighbouring Island. Hindostan has an abundant population which Ceylon has not. Hindostan is a grain-exporting country; while Ceylon has, from remote ages, imported grain for those adventurers who have made it their temporary abode for the improvement of their fortunes.

The only resemblance in the economy of England to that of Ceylon is, that both countries import grain; but the causes which lead to such importations in the one, are as opposite to

---

* Surely those who are in embarrassed circumstances, in consequence of their own improvidence, are the last men—no matter how high their political standing—who should be entrusted with the disposal of the revenues of Indian possessions.

† See Stouart on the Monetary System of Ceylon.

those which produce them in the other, as they well can be.
In England the study of statesmen is to find employment for
the poor; while in Ceylon the difficulty is to find poor to employ. England has not sufficient land to produce food for its
manufacturing people; while Ceylon has not sufficient labouring population to cultivate the soil for English capitalists,
and has none to spare for manufacturing purposes. England
always had a considerable pauper population; while Ceylon
was without paupers until the attempt was made to govern it
as an English colony instead of as an Indian possession.

The inhabitants of Ceylon cannot be displaced by English
colonists, as is the case in the colonies planted in Australia,
where the colonists have carried with them the institutions of
the mother country, and where they may be left to govern
themselves as long as England reserves the power to protect
the poor when oppressed by their wealthy fellow-colonists.
Nor can the Ceylonese be exterminated as the Caribbeans are
said to have been in the West Indies. They are too far advanced in civilization to retreat, like the Veddahs, into the
forests of the interior; their rights and usages have been
solemnly acknowledged by three successive European governments, and, as the climate does not admit of the employment
of European labourers, it is sound policy as well as Christian
duty to treat them with justice and forbearance. Such treat-
ment can only be insured by the reins of government being
held by European officers of administrative ability, responsible to England for the faithful discharge of their duty; and
certainly not in any degree left to persons—no matter how
respectable—who are not in the paid service of, and responsible
to, the State.

The liquidation of the temporary debt incurred on account
of the expenses attending the suppression of the rebellion in
1848, and the injurious effect on the revenue occasioned by
that event, as well as by the severe check given to planting
and commercial speculations by the monetary crisis of 1847,
induced the Governor to enforce considerable economy in the

L

public expenditure. His Excellency's prudent retrenchments on public works disappointed the expectations of the planters and merchants; and, as the revenue was insufficient to meet their requirements, some of them called for reductions in official salaries and for the abolition of certain offices, among which was that of the Treasury, and proposed that the public cash in its vaults should be handed over to the custody of the Bank. It was not, however, until sufficient time had elapsed for the recovery of confidence and the expansion of trade, that a Committee commenced its deliberations on a state of affairs which had nearly ceased to exist.

The following extracts are taken from some observations which were called forth by the proceedings of this Committee:—

" In order to provide an efficient remedy for any evil, it is necessary never to lose sight of the causes which have led to it, even should it be impossible to remove those causes.

" There is no country so very poor as not to possess within itself sufficient means, under judicious management, for its own gradual social advancement and worldly prosperity. It is as true of nations as of individuals, that they may be over stimulated by the repletion of capital and of luxury. It is generally found that whenever the commerce of a country flourishes, the value of money decreases within that country in comparison with that of property and the necessaries of life. But as commercial prosperity is generally beneficial to the inhabitants and to the revenue, both the Government and the people, with few exceptions, are prepared to meet without inconvenience the usual diminution in the value of money occasioned by its increasing abundance. Such being the consequences of sound fiscal regulations, similar results would follow in Ceylon if its system of revenue were established on sound principles. Previous to the check given to commercial prosperity in 1848—the effect of which has nearly passed away—the large sums received from England for expenditure on coffee plantations, and the commercial profits resulting from such speculations, were amply sufficient to enable those who received them to meet the enormous increase in the cost of all things. Nevertheless, the Government has not revenue in proportion to meet the increased cost of public works, nor to raise the salaries of its servants to meet the increased expenditure for the necessary maintenance of their families. With these facts before us we have the astounding anomaly of a Committee devising means for a reduction of official salaries, instead of increasing the revenue in order to raise those of the lower scale, which increase is imperatively called for.

"In a small European community such as that of Colombo, which is chiefly composed of merchants and planters, it is impossible to be unacquainted with their prevailing opinion,— that the tolls on the high roads, and the import duty on the rice consumed by their immigrant coolies, are sufficient imposts to be borne by the planters. But it should be remembered that the payment of tolls on the high road existed before coffee plantations were commenced, and that their payment is in exact proportion to the use that is made of such roads by the payers; and, even if the import duty on rice were lowered, it would not be possible to obtain immigrant coolie labour on easier terms than now. In truth, there is no country in the world where the producers and exporters of produce contribute so little towards the support of the State, in proportion to their incomes, as those highly favoured individuals in Ceylon.

"In the majority of districts where the grain-producing lands are private property, the cultivators contribute a tithe of their produce to the Government ; but there are other districts in which, the land being Crown property, the cultivators contribute nearly one-half of their produce in lieu of rent. The sooner all grain-producing lands become private property, and their produce subject to one uniform tax, the better. Europeans will never cultivate rice on the disadvantageous terms imposed on some of the Singhalese cultivators ; nor is it to be expected that these poor people will continue to do so

much longer. It may be seen in 'Bertolacci,' page 203, that
he was of opinion that the cultivation of rice should be protected by a higher duty than one per cent. import duty, which
was levied in his time. Subsequent rulers have adopted his
view, and the duty is at present sevenpence per bushel, which
—now that grain is so dear—is equal to twelve per cent. *ad
valorem*; and when the sevenpenny rate was originally adopted
it was equal to fifteen per cent. : but it has not had the effect
of inducing the Ceylonese to increase the cultivation, nor
Europeans to do so for the supply of their immigrant coolies,
and its imports from India are considerably on the increase.
That these imports are promptly paid for, is a clear demon-
stration of the important fact, that the Ceylonese find employment more profitable than that of growing rice; and that
while labour is at its present cost, and they can obtain more
money by producing articles for exportation, it is not to be
expected of them, any more than of European planters, that
they should increase the cultivation of grain. Such being the
case, and the Government greatly in want of revenue, there is
no sufficient reason for the total repeal of the import duty on
grain; but it should not exceed the rate contributed by the
Ceylon cultivator : and, for the sake of those persons whose
incomes do not increase with commercial prosperity and the
decreasing value of money, it would be desirable to lower it
to the general rate fixed on other imports for revenue purposes. As taxation cannot be brought home to the mass of
the people without imposts on arrack, salt, and grain, it is
wise to continue import duty on rice, notwithstanding it is
wise to admit corn duty free into England.

" If sufficient time be allowed, and no Imperial act should
have a lowering effect on the prices of produce, the revenue of
Ceylon will soon become ample for all necessary purposes ; but
if more revenue must be had without delay, then it should be
obtained through the medium of the Custom-house; otherwise a tax on all incomes above £300 a year would effect the
desired reduction in official salaries, as well as insure to the

State some share in the increasing profits of commercial and planting speculations. But the re-establishment of a moderate scale of export duties should not under any circumstances be delayed. In Ceylon the advantages of an export duty consist in the ease with which it is collected at the Custom-house, and its direct action on that part only of a planter's property on which he obtains his profit. It is in truth the perfection of an income or property-tax, or even of a land-tax, because it is fair and equitable on all persons without being inquisitorial. It is, moreover, not levied until the produce has become convertible into money by means of Bills of Exchange drawn against its proceeds.

The difficulties of the Government of Ceylon, resulting from the establishment of the system of colonial government in and over an Indian possession, have been increased by so many of its officers becoming planters, and their having necessarily to enter into the commercial details which such occupation involves. It is thus that their interest has become so identical with that of English planters and merchants, as to produce that preponderating influence in the Councils which has led to that kind of legislation and those governmental measures which are only suited to colonies properly so called. In general conversation, in speeches upon public occasions, and in the tone of the local press—the feather which indicates the direction of the European popular breeze-it is the success of the COLONY, that is the almost universal theme. If the name of Ceylon should happen accidentally to be mentioned, it will be found that the subject relates to the prosperity of the sojourners, or to the increase of revenue and its applicability to commercial facilities; but as regards the welfare and happiness of the *Ceylonese* all are as silent as midnight on Pedrotalla galla! * Even the rulers of the land estimate the importance of a district by the amount of its revenue rather

* The highest land in Ceylon

than by the number of its inhabitants; and the ability of the officer in charge is estimated by the amount of his collections rather than by the happiness of the people entrusted to his care. In fact, the proceedings of the Government have appeared to resemble those of landlords of the soil rather than rulers of people. But these evils would be increased by any addition to the number of unofficial members in the Legislative Council before there are native gentlemen, independent of all connexion with Government or with trade, emulous of seats in that Assembly, and the people of the country are sufficiently instructed to appreciate the advantages of such liberal institutions. What can be a more convincing proof of the preponderating influence of the European community, than their present clamour for a railroad for their commercial convenience between Colombo and Kandy; and that the revenue of the whole Island should be pledged to guarantee certain profit to the shareholders? This monstrous proposition to tax a whole community for the convenience of a very few, is attempted to be justified by what is being done in India, where the object of the East India Company is the political advantage insured by the speedy transmission of troops, and where the tenure of the Government is by no means so secure as that of the Crown in Ceylon, where political objects are comparatively insignificant. The same may be said in respect to the call for Government interference in obtaining immigrant coolies at the cost of the general revenue, when it is well known that the chief cause of the want of labour from the neighbouring coast is the uncertainty attending the payment of the coolies on those plantations where the proprietors are in want of money, and that if payment be made certain on *all* plantations there will be no want of coolies. It may be necessary for this Government to assure that of Madras that the emigrants from that Presidency shall receive its protection and enjoy all the benefits common to the people of Ceylon; but further than this any Government interference would be injurious, even to the planting community : for if these energetic Englishmen be left to their own exertions they will successfully overcome all impediments, and be all the happier under a system of government which in all its measures looks to the general happiness of all instead of to the special benefit of any particular class. All that enterprising Englishmen require to insure their success is fair play and no special favours.

"In 1833, when perfect freedom was proclaimed by Royal authority to the inhabitants of Ceylon, the Civil Service was thrown open to all qualified persons. It was also proclaimed that the Civil Service should henceforth consist of offices, and no longer be one of the names of men! As an exclusive Civil Service was incompatible with perfect freedom to all classes, this great change appeared to be consistent; but notwithstanding this Royal boon conferred on the community has never been publicly annulled, the Civil Service of Ceylon has become almost as exclusive as ever. It is, however, a question for grave consideration, whether it would not be wise to refrain from measures which have a tendency to promote the amalgamation of races, or to infringe those bounds which the Creator, for his own wise purposes, has made so distinct. At any rate, until Europeans and natives associate in trading and planting co-partnership, of which there is no instance at present, it must be a very questionable proceeding to raise one or two native youths to the governing branch of the Civil Service. It would no doubt be highly gratifying to the fortunate individuals so elevated; but would it be a happy measure, or calculated to be approved by the people, particularly by the elderly Modeliers? A young native, on becoming a writer in the Civil Service, may have to do duty as an Assistant Government Agent, and thus become the superior officer of the elderly Modelier of the Cutcherry; who may be of higher birth, and who is possessed of the experience necessary to be the adviser of the Government Agent. Surely in a country where pride of birth is so strong, such a proceeding would prove to be a source of ill-feeling incompatible with official harmony. If the time had arrived when the reins of government should be entrusted to native hands, it would be more wise to entrust them to such intelligent and experienced native gentlemen as Modelier De Lowera, of the Colombo Cutcherry, than to run the chance of such qualities being found in his or any other Modelier's *sons*. Twenty years have not yet passed since Rajah-Karia was abolished on account of the abuse it was subject to in its exercise by native chiefs and headmen. Is it reasonable to expect that power to rule over men may be safely entrusted to the sons of those who were charged with its abuse in 1833 ? Would it not be more prudent and equally just towards the natives, if the importance, responsibilities, and salaries of the Modeliers and other headmen were increased? It is now the practice for every Government Agent in charge of a province or district to be assisted by a Modelier, through whom all orders are issued to the people. Would it not be attended with gratification to the inhabitants, and ensure their satisfaction with the orders of the Government Agent, if the Modelier stood towards the Government Agent in a similar relation to that in which members of the Executive Council stood towards the Governor previous to 1833,—that they should be consulted on all measures relating to the government of the province, and possess the right of protest against being responsible for such measures as they did not approve, in order that the Government might become aware of their disapproval ? By thus raising the native Civil Service in a comparative degree with that of the European, satisfaction would be given to the natives, and a salutary check imposed on European administrators of affairs in distant provinces and districts. Surely such proceeding would not only raise the position of the Modeliers, but would stimulate their sons and the rising generation in general to qualify themselves for such advancement ; and be attended with much happier results than the amalgamation of a very few native youths with the governing branch of the European Civil Service.

" Even as the reins of government in the several provinces and districts should be exclusively held by English gentlemen possessed of the best administrative ability in the public service, so should the Bench of the Supreme Court and the office of Queen's Advocate be invariably filled by barristers sent out expressly from England, in order that they may be perfectly free from all local connexions and associations. But as the decisions of the District Courts, and of all the other minor tribunals, are subject to the appellant jurisdiction of the Supreme Court, these minor benches may be safely occupied by aspirants from the Ceylon Bar, appointed by the Governor and approved by the Judges of the Supreme Court. But these aspirants should be Christian gentlemen;—for the apostle, St. Paul, enjoins his converts not to appeal to heathen Judges, and therefore it cannot be right in a Christian Government to appoint heathen magistrates to preside in judgment over Christians. The Dutch excluded all who were not Christians from the service of Government; but this practice was highly objectionable, as it no doubt made many hypocrites: but hypocrisy is not to be apprehended of honourable gentlemen learned in the law.

The salaries of the minor Courts of Justice should be sufficient to induce the members of the Ceylon Bar to aspire to the benches; and when filled by English gentlemen they should be contented with the same amount of salary. As a general rule, there are advantages in having trained lawyers to preside in these courts; but it does not follow that educated English gentlemen, who have not been trained to the law, are not equal to all the duties of a district court. The knowledge of Ceylon law is as readily acquired by an educated writer sent from England, as by a Ceylonese youth articled to a proctor for that single purpose. Some of the best provincial and district Judges commenced their Ceylon career as writers in the Civil Service, and others as officers in the army.

" It is to be regretted that the waste lands near the sea and inland waters on which cocoa-nut trees would flourish had not become the private property of the natives of these places before the demand for cocoa-nut oil and other produce of these

M

Palms had rendered these possessions too valuable for poor natives to become their purchasers, as, at the present upset price, they will in all probability become the property of English capitalists, who, in the absence of an export duty or other property-tax, will enjoy their revenues in England and contribute comparatively nothing towards the support of the Government of Ceylon, nor towards the education and civilization of the natives of the Island, which on Christian gentlemen is a duty equally imperative."

CHAPTER XIV.

Proposed Removal of the Steam-packet Station from Galle to Trinco-
malie—Proposed Railroad from Colombo to Trincomalie—Advantages
of a Public Debt—Memorial in favour of Government retaining the
Manufacture and Issue of Paper Currency—The advantage of Treasury
Notes in defraying the Cost of a Railway—Public Defalcations—Their
Remedy—Close of Sir George Anderson's Administration.

SOMETIME in the year 1853, the Peninsular and Oriental Steam
Navigation Company applied to the Lords Commissioners of
the Admiralty to be allowed to substitute the Port of Trincomalie for that of Point de Galle as the station for disembarking mails and passengers. In the remonstrance against
this concession it was stated, that as the shoals and rocks in
the harbour of Point de Galle had not increased, and as the
anchorage was not so much exposed to the monsoon winds as
the roadstead of Madras, it appeared that the principal object
of the Peninsular and Oriental Steam Navigation Company in
making this request must be their desire to have but one
coaling station between Aden and Calcutta, which the increased tonnage of their steamers would enable them to accomplish if the Port of Trincomalie were made that one; but
that if the mails and passengers for Ceylon were to be landed
and received at Trincomalie, it would be seriously inconvenient
to the Government, and especially so to the commercial community, to whom serious losses might result from the delay in
the delivery of the English mails; that Trincomalie is 327 sea
miles beyond Point de Galle, and distant from Colombo by
land 185 miles,—of which the mails, if conveyed across the
Island, would have to be carried 113 by coolies; and, if conveyed the whole distance by sea, would have to pass over 587
miles,—which would involve a delay in their delivery at Colombo of about 66 hours, or three days, in a steamer running

at the rate of nine miles an hour. That if it should be resolved
to abandon Point de Galle as a coaling station, the mails from
England might be landed at Colombo with but very little
delay to the steamers, as the distance from Aden to Point de
Galle or Trincomalie would only be increased 21 miles by
their calling off Colombo to land the mails. That during the
past seven years the Government has been repeatedly solicited
by a Company of railway speculators to guarantee them a
certain profit on the amount they may expend in making a
railway between Colombo and Kandy, but for making such
railroad there exists no governmental or political reason whatever; and, therefore, the pledging of the revenue raised from
the inhabitants of all parts of the Island for the benefit of
those only who are interested in the Central Province, could
not be equitably maintained: but if the English mails should
be landed at Trincomalie, the making of a railway from Colombo to that port would be an undertaking of much political.
importance. It would connect the capital—the seat of the
Government and of commerce—with the principal Royal naval
depôt. For such a purpose the general revenue of the Island
could not be misapplied. It would manifestly be more wise
to retain the right of property in the railroad than that it
should become that of speculators, who would be sure to
require full payment of the interest guaranteed to them, and
which would fall heavier on the revenue of the Island than
interest on a loan raised for the purpose of making a railroad
on account of the State, after deducting the traffic receipts.*

When the debentures which had been issued to raise money
to defray the expenses of the Kandian war of 1818 were paid
off, the Governor of Ceylon was forbidden to contract any
future public debt: but for the purpose of assisting the revenue in the completion of a *single line* of rail across the Island
for the conveyance of the English mails, such restrictions on

* See note at the end of this Chapter.

His Excellency might prudently be withdrawn. Such a public debt would afford the means of secure investment for trust-money, and the funds belonging to widows and orphans, as well as those for the support of the aged and helpless. Ceylon has no such secure means of investment; and, as no portion of its people are more entitled to the protection of the Government than those who are unable to protect themselves, tho sooner it is provided with such means the nearer will its Rulers be to the fulfilment of their duty.

In 1854 an Ordinance to amend the law relating to bank-ing was suspended pending a reference to England of the following Memorial :—

> " The Memorial of James Steuart, to His Excellency tho Governor, and the Honourable the Members of tho Legislative Council,

" Respectfully showeth,

" That your Memorialist conceives it to be his duty to avail himself of the opportunity which is afforded by your attention being directed to the amendment of the law relating to the business of Bankers in Ceylon, to submit a few brief observa-tions upon this most important proposition,—the principal feature of which is the extension of the privilege now enjoyed by Bankers, and by no other traders in Ceylon,—that of issuing unstamped notes amounting to ten shillings and upwards.

" Your Memorialist is wholly at a loss to conceive how such privilege can be extended consistently with the spirit of the age, the principles of free-trade, as opposed to monopoly of every description; the perfect equality in trade, whether it be in money or in merchandise, and the great financial principles enunciated by the late Mr. Huskisson and Sir Robert Peel, and supported by Earl Grey and the first financiers and statesmen of modern times. Your Memorialist believes that the Oriental Bank has recently obtained a Charter from the Imperial Government. But as such Charter has not been published in

Ceylon, ninety-nine persons out of every hundred of the inhabitants are ignorant of the fact, that the shareholders in that establishment are not liable for its debts, in the same manner as they were before they obtained their Charter, and in the same manner as all individual shareholders in all the other commercial companies in the Island are at this time. It is most difficult to understand why a company of traders in money should enjoy a right of sovereignty gratuitously conferred upon it, which is forbidden to all other traders, both companies and individuals, not denominated Bankers. Your Memorialist is aware that the proper business of Bankers does not expose them to that risk from losses in trade to which other commercial companies are liable; and while Banks confine themselves to their legitimate business of dealing in gold and silver, receiving deposits, and advancing on convertible securities, the more there are of them the better for the rest of the community, just as may be said of merchants and dealers of every description. But this chartered institution gives and takes bills on distant countries on its own account, which is beyond all doubt the business of merchants and cambists, and not that of Bankers. In its dealings in exchanges it is as liable to losses as any commercial establishment; and this alone, independent of the principles of free-trade, should have disentitled it to a Charter of limited liability and to the privilege of issuing paper money. In the absence of a full knowledge of the provisions of its Charter, your Memorialist cannot conceive how it can confer the privilege of issuing paper money; for such privilege the Bank of England pays a valuable consideration to the State, and even that corporation—if newspaper reports can be depended on—has recently received an intimation from a Secretary of State, that Government may deem it expedient to establish a Royal Bank, and resume the sovereign right of supplying paper, as it does metallic, currency to the people. It is of the first importance that coining and all regulations concerning current money should, as they do, fall strictly within the functions of Government; since if these objects are neglected, the property of individuals may be put in jeopardy every day. But on this subject Earl Grey has forcibly expressed his opinion to the Governor of New Zealand in the following words:—' The business of banking, or of dealing in money, and that of issuing paper money, I consider to have not merely no necessary but no proper connexion with each other. The former is a branch of commercial business which should be left, like every other, to private enterprise. But to issue money, that is to furnish the authorized medium of exchange, is one of the peculiar, and not the least important, functions of Government. With respect to the coinage, this principle has always been ˈrecognized; nor is there any attribute of sovereignty which has been more strongly insisted upon and more rigidly guarded from invasion by the supreme authority of almost every State, whether of ancient or modern times, than the exclusive right of coining money for the use of its own subjects. As to the issue of paper money, a different rule has generally been followed; but, as experience has proved, with the very worst result. By allowing the issue of paper money to become a commercial speculation, the amount issued from time to time has been made to vary, not according to the real wants of the community, but according to the interest of the issuer'.

"Your Memorialist is however of opinion, that if, on account of some political or State reason, Government should resolve on ceasing to issue paper money, such privilege should be disposed of for the highest consideration to *one* properly constituted Bank, with proper provisions for public safety, securing for the benefit of the State all the profits or economy which paper money affords; for to have more than one place for the making and issuing paper money is as objectionable as it would be to employ more than one mint for the making and issuing of metallic money; the end or object being in both cases the same—to preserve an invariable standard by which services can be calculated and commodities and the necessaries of life interchanged—for such things are not parted with *for* money, but *by* money *for* each other. It is admitted on the principles of free-trade, that the less trade is fettered, and the more that can be obtained of any given commodity for any given service the better for the public good; but in money, which is the measure, the object to be aimed at is not *quantity*, but *certainty* and steadiness, which never will be found by competition in the issue of paper money.

"Your Memorialist is of opinion, that there is no country where it is more necessary to prevent fluctuation in prices than Ceylon. The price of labour and of the necessaries of life are now higher than the value of the exportable produce of the soil can well bear, when brought into competition with that of other countries; and the greater the facilities become for issuing paper money, the greater will be the depression in its value, and the higher will become the prices of all necessaries of life and the cost of exportable produce; and the greater the embarrassment of planting and commercial operations.

"Your Memorialist believes that the value and importance of the sovereign right to supply the community with paper currency would be most clearly perceived, were the Government of Ceylon to resolve on raising a loan for the formation of a railroad; for the more paper money it could keep in circulation, the less would be the amount necessary to raise on loan, and the less would be the revenue required to pay the interest upon such loan: whereas, by allowing a Bank to make and issue paper money without giving complete indemnification to the State, the Government is not only deprived of such advantageous use of its paper money, but a benefit equivalent to a loan without interest is conferred upon the Bank shareholders at the expense of the whole community.

"In conclusion, your Memorialist prays, that the consideration of your Honourable Council may be given to the propriety of the Government resuming the sole right of making and issuing paper money, or that it should dispose of such exclusive privilege for the highest consideration to one properly constituted Bank.

"Your Memorialist, as in duty bound, will ever pray,

"JAMES STEUART.

" Colombo, 19th of December, 1854."

This Memorial was referred by the Secretary of State to the Lords Commissioners of Her Majesty's Treasury, and on its prayer being deemed inexpedient by their Lordship's financial Secretary,* the Banks obtained the victory, and the Ordinance in their favour became the law of Ceylon.

In order to perceive the full extent of the mischief which might result from such concessions, let it be supposed that the Rulers of Ceylon should yield to the English commercial entreaty and grant a guaranteed rate of 6 per cent. interest to shareholders in a railway, abolish the Treasury, withdraw all its notes from circulation, and transfer the public cash from its vaults to the coffers of one of the Banks. Would not the increased circulation of Bank notes, consequent on the withdrawal of those of the Treasury and the transferred cash balances, afford increased facilities to the shareholders and customers of the Banks to purchase railway scrip, on which the Ceylonese, through their Rulers, would be bound to pay

---

* This Right Honourable gentleman, on being subsequently appointed a member of the Supreme Council of India, proceeded to Calcutta, and very soon perceived that measures which he deemed inexpedient when in London were not only expedient but necessary in India. His monetary scheme for that Empire embraces all that was prayed for in the Memorial from Ceylon, and, as a whole, is precisely the same as the system which existed in that Island before the Banks were permitted to issue paper currency; for the Treasury of Ceylon issued the only paper currency, and its notes were convertible into cash at the Cutcherries of the several provinces throughout the Island.

6 per cent. interest? When schoolboys act in this way they are said by their fellows "to give stones to break their own heads."

The general result of English rule in Ceylon may be considered to have proved that the salaries of the Civil Service have been sufficient to ensure personal integrity in its members; nevertheless, there have been considerable money defalcations, resulting from too much dependence being placed on subordinate officials, whose salaries have not been sufficient to prevent their yielding to the great temptation which is afforded by the absence of that close attention which a faulty system renders necessary in principal officers.

Before 1833, there was a Paymaster-General, who kept open accounts with all the public departments, as well as special accounts of expenditure upon all estimates sanctioned or warranted by the Governor; by these means this officer could effectually prevent any account from being overdrawn, as no money could be advanced or paid by the Treasurer without an order from the Paymaster-General. With a view to retrenchment of the public expenditure, these responsible duties of Paymaster-General were imposed on the Treasurer, and thereby a most salutary check on his payments destroyed; which has opened the door for those money defalcations which have taken place in several departments. If the saving of the salary of Paymaster-General was necessary, his duties should have been transferred to the Auditor-General; whose office would then have become a check on improper demands before they were made on the Treasury. It would then have been the duty of the Auditor-General to have ascertained the correctness of an account before it was paid, instead of his doing so long afterwards when arranging the general accounts of the Island for final audit in England; in other words, locking the stable door after the horse has been stolen. The sooner this change is effected, and the duties and responsibilities of the Treasurer are shared by the Auditor-General, the better; for, with the exception of the services of the latter officer in the

Councils of Government, there is no one so well paid who has
so little to do, and that little so simple in its nature. An
Auditor-General would be a most useful officer if he were converted into a Clerk of the Cheque on all irregular proceedings,
and it were his duty to bring them to the notice of the Governor as he now does an error of a farthing in the addition
of an account after it has been paid.

When Sir George Anderson had realized the peculiar difficulties of his position, as the Ruler of an Indian possession
under the Colonial system of Government, his desire to work
out this most difficult political problem became evident; but
unfortunately his health failed just when his energies were
most needed to restrain the preponderating demands of his
own countrymen for a guarantee to be given to the shareholders in a Railway Company, and for increased expenditure
on those public works in which they took interest. Under
these circumstances, His Excellency's departure from Ceylon
was not regretted by the English in a corresponding degree
with the welcome they gave him on his arrival. Nevertheless,
the Administration of Sir George Anderson conferred benefit
on the people; and had his health been spared to carry out
his own views for the good of all classes, that benefit would
have become more unmistakeably conspicuous. He left Ceylon
a confirmed invalid, with his family, on the 18th of January,
1855, and the charge of the Island devolved on the Honourable
C. J. MacCarthy, Esquire, as Lieutenant-Governor, until the
arrival of Sir Henry George Ward, on the 11th of May,
1855.

NOTE.

In a Despatch from the Governor of Ceylon, addressed to the
Secretary of State, published in the *Overland Ceylon Times, July,*
1862, it appears that the existing desire of the Peninsular and
Oriental Steam Navigation Company to adopt the Port of Trincomalie as a coaling station, instead of that of Point de Galle, is
objected to by the local Government, and that His Excellency, with
his usual ability, has enumerated the serious objections to the proposed change as regards the transmission of mails and passengers

across the Island. It would, however, be as well to remind those persons who desire that Trincomalie should become the coaling station, of the want of anchorage ground off the entrance, and within the great bay of that Port; also of the strong southerly current which sets past it in the N.E. monsoon—all of which are grave objections to that harbour as a resort for colliers and other sailing vessels; and further, that commercial men should bear in mind that the wet season on the eastern coast of Ceylon is at that period of the year when dry weather is required for preparing the coffee for shipment, as it is now prepared and shipped at Colombo.

It further appears, that the Governor is unwilling to advocate a single line of railway to Trincomalie, as suggested in my Report to the late Sir George Anderson, in 1854, and that the Admiralty discourage my suggestion, in the same Report, that the steam-packets should call off Colombo for the purpose of embarking and disembarking mails and passengers, " on the grounds that the anchorage at Colombo is open, and in the S.W. monsoon both inconvenient and dangerous; that the steamers, owing to their large draught of water, would be compelled to be a mile and a half off shore, and that boats would be obliged to pass a turbulent bar in landing mails and passengers."

With respect to the Governor's disinclination to advocate a single line of railway to Trincomalie, I can only say that His Excellency should be a better judge respecting the *political* and commercial advantages of such a means of communication, and the purely commercial advantage of a railway between Colombo and Kandy. But after thirty years' residence as Master Attendant at Colombo, and experience previously gained in command of merchant ships trading to Ceylon, I feel that I should not refrain from expressing my professional opinion on the anchorage of that Port; and on the facilities afforded for the embarkation and disembarkation of mails and passengers from steam-packets calling there for the purpose.

Master mariners, bound for Colombo, anchor there at all seasons, in from 7 to 8½ fathoms water, which is from one-third to one-half of a mile from the rocky point on which the Custom-house stands, and which protects the anchorage for coasting vessels and the landing place for boats. Beyond the anchorage ground usually occupied by merchant ships—in from 8 to 10 fathoms, about three-quarters of a mile from the point—the holding ground is so exceedingly tenacious that anchors and cables have been broken in getting under weigh. This muddy space is produced by the sediment from the stream which issues from " Calany ganga" in the rainy season—a stream which lessens the strain on ships' cables in the S.W. monsoon. " The anchorage at Colombo is open"—so is the anchorage in Torbay, and in many other roadsteads which are frequented by shipping. Our

fishing smacks ride on the Dogger Bank, and ships of war have rode
out winter gales in the North Sea and on the western coast of France,
from Ushant nearly to Bayonne, exposed to the ocean's waves, and
to such heavy gales as shipping do not experience at Colombo.
Even the strong winds of the S.W. monsoon seldom blow home,
except in squalls. It is true that, at intervals of from fourteen to
seventeen years, the southern margin of the cyclones, which are felt
in the Bay of Bengal, and sometimes at Jaffnapatam in the early
part of the N.E. monsoon, have been felt for a few hours at Colombo,
to the injury of unprepared shipping; but those well found with
ground tackling—that ground tackling kept in good order, and timely
availed of—have nothing to fear when at anchor in Colombo roads.
Trained up to believe, what experience has confirmed, that ships
properly provided with anchors and cables are as safe at anchor on
good holding ground as in any other position exposed to the ocean's
waves, I was not prepared for these objections on the part of the
Admiralty, notwithstanding the prevailing desire for artificial har-
bours of refuge, which—since the great improvement in the means
of weighing heavier anchors than were formerly in use—are becoming
less and less necessary.

"That boats would be obliged to pass a turbulent bar in landing mails and passengers." There are times when landing at Colombo in ships' boats, in charge of persons unacquainted with
the bar, is attended with danger; but such is not the case in
boats belonging to the Port, when conducted by the local pilots
and steersmen who are in the habit of crossing the bar in all
weathers.

When I suggested that the steam-packets should call off Colombo,
I contemplated building boats of safe construction expressly for the
purpose; and if I had been aware of the objections entertained by
the Admiralty, I should have suggested to the Governor of Ceylon,
that rather than have to convey the mails to and from Trincomalie
without a single line of railway, it would be well to moor a vessel to
receive the mails off Colombo at sufficient distance for the steam-
packets to keep under weigh during their transmission from one
vessel to the other. This would be attended with some expense, but
only for the short time necessary to give confidence to the officers of
the steam-packets; who, on seeing the facility with which the boats
proceeded direct to the shore with the mails and passengers, instead
of depositing them on board the vessel moored for the purpose of
receiving them, would soon become convinced that such vessel could
be dispensed with.

Since the 97th Regiment were (in opposition to the wishes of the
Governor) landed at Trincomalie, in 1825, from the Honourable East
India Company's ships that had brought them from England, and

were subsequently subjected to a tedious passage of many weeks against the S.W. monsoon, on their way to Colombo in ships hired by the local Government for the purpose, all troops, except those employed to garrison Trincomalie, have been disembarked at Colombo at all seasons, and that—so far as my memory serves me—without the least delay occasioned by stress of weather.

J. S.

CHAPTER XV.

On the Improvement of the Cattle and Sheep of Ceylon.*

COMMERCE is defined by McCullock to be "the exchange of commodities for commodities," or the exchange of the produce of one country for that of another. Now, although this definition is undisputed, it is nevertheless remarkable, that in this commercial age, when all persons admit the great importance of commerce, that there should exist such a strong desire in almost all civilized countries to render the inhabitants independent of commerce, by inciting them to endeavour to produce on their own soil all the necessaries and luxuries of life which they import from other States. This desire, if succeeded in, would destroy commercial intercourse between nations, and check the advancement of civilization and the extension of Christianity. But it hath pleased the Omnipotent to fix limits to the accomplishment of men's desires, by restricting particular productions to particular countries, each possessing some product of peculiar excellence which insures its intercourse with other nations. In these providential arrangements we may perceive that it is the intention of the All-wise God to promote commercial intercourse between all the nations and peoples of this beautiful world; and that those who engage in commerce should also be the pioneers of civilization and Christianity to all mankind. Were it not for these determinate limits, those persons who make it their study and endeavour to produce all things within their own country would become unsocial, if not selfish, neighbours. But as it

---

* Written at Nuwera-Ellia in August, 1853.

is, many of them waste their time and money in vain endeavours to cultivate foreign productions, instead of confining
their attention to the more profitable improvement of the productions of their own country, which its soil, its climate, its
people, and its other peculiar qualities, are by nature adapted
to bring to the greatest perfection. There are, of course, exceptions to these general observations; and the coffee plant in
Ceylon may be instanced as one. It is, however, by no means
an ascertained fact, that the coffee plant is not, like those of
cotton and tea, indigenous. Be this as it may, we now find
that it is more wise to improve the culture of coffee than to
waste a thought upon the culture of either cotton or tea; nor
should we, for similar reasons, lament our own inability to
grow sufficient rice for our increasing sojourning inhabitants :
because, like cotton and tea, rice can be produced cheaper in
other countries, where labour is more abundant. There can
be no surer sign of a people's prosperity than their being able
to pay those of other countries to provide them with abundance of food; and this must be the case with the Ceylonese,
or their importations of grain would very soon diminish. All
the time that our imports consist of those things which are
not produced in Ceylon, or are not produced in sufficient
quantity, or of equal quality, and while our imports are
promptly paid for, there can be no reason to doubt the
prosperity of the people or the general discretion of their
rulers. But when the imports are of inferior quality to the
natural productions of the country,—like the cattle and sheep
now being imported from Hindostan,—it then becomes a
matter for serious consideration, whether such a state of things
cannot be remedied; and therefore it is the object of this
paper to call attention to the improvement of the horned cattle
and the sheep of this Island.

Ceylon is, by nature, provided with a breed of cattle much
better suited to its climate and roads than any that can be
imported. Its small, compact, hardy, black cattle—now becoming extinct—are not only good for food, but they are the

best for draft purposes, and should be preserved for the conveyance of rice and coffee to and from the interior. Now, although sheep do not thrive on the herbage of the southern provinces, and the leeches of the Kandian country—except it be above the elevation suited for the culture of coffee—prevent their being reared with success in the central province, no country has sheep better adapted to its climate than the Jaffna sheep are to the northern province; nor is the mutton of a well-fed Jaffna wether surpassed by that of any imported sheep. Jaffna sheep not being provided with wool to enable them to withstand the cold at Nuwera-Ellia, it may be desirable to import some with sufficient natural covering to keep them warm at such high elevation. But for no other purpose would it be necessary to import either cattle or sheep if the natives were properly instructed by English graziers in the improved method of breeding, rearing, and preparing the natural breeds of the Island,—the horned cattle for draft and the Jaffna sheep for the table. The money that has been fruitlessly expended on the importations of sheep from Aden, Bengal, Coimbetore, the Cape, and England, would have paid for a skilful English grazier's visit to Ceylon for the purpose of instructing the Ceylonese in his new art.

CHAPTER XVI.

Buddhism in Ceylon—Caste—Missionary labours.

EXTRACTS from the "Notes on Buddhism," by the Rev. D. J. Gogerly; appended to George Lee's translation of Ribeyro's History of Ceylon :—

" ' The Buddhas are incomprehensible ; their doctrines are incomprehensible ; and the fruits of faith to those who have faith in these incomprehensibles are also incomprehensible.' " —(From the "Mahawanso," Chap. xvii.)

" The origin of Buddhism is lost in remote antiquity ; for although the era of Goutama, the last Buddha, has been ascertained with considerable accuracy, yet the whole of the sacred books declare that he merely revived a system which had previously existed, the doctrines of which had ceased to be known."

Goutama declares " that, at the time he assumed the title of Buddha, no trace of the doctrines taught by his predecessors could be found ; and that he, by his own unaided mental powers, had re-discovered the whole." He places the periods of existence of previous Buddahs " in incredibly remote ages." It is inferred "that the doctrines of" the early Buddhas "had not altogether become extinct from the circumstance, that other sects affirmed that their doctrines and those of Goutama were identical. He denies the correctness of their assertion, and points out the difference ;" " but the explanations" "turn on such minute metaphysical distinctions as to show that a general resemblance existed."

" Buddhism is not so much a religion as a school of philosophy. Buddha acknowledged no Supreme Being,—no one who can justly claim adoration and obedience from all. The only supremacy acknowledged or taught by him is, the supremacy of virtue and wisdom : for, according to his doctrine, these are inseparably united, so that no truly wise man can be vicious ; if he be so, his professed wisdom can only be respecting subjects of little importance ; and in reference to the higher paths of knowledge his vice proves his ignorance : and, on the same principle, although a man may be ignorant of many things, yet if his conduct be virtuous his virtue proves him to be possessed of the highest style of wisdom. He taught that the virtuous man should be honoured, especially by those who had not made equal progress in excellency : and as he affirmed himself to have attained to the perfection of virtue, and to be possessed of universal and unerring knowledge, he claimed homage from all, and had to render it to none." The homage claimed by him " is mental reverence, indicated by the external gesture of bowing the body, and by the presenting such gifts or offerings as might minister to the comfort of the superior ; who received them not from a desire of gratification, all his desires having become extinct, but that the individuals who presented them might obtain the reward of virtue. In all offerings, therefore, a formula was either expressed or understood, — ' Lord, compassionate me, and receive this my offering.' "

" Although Buddha, as the highest, is entitled to receive this homage from all, yet each being, in proportion to his virtue, is entitled to respect and homage, similar in kind to that offered to Buddha, from those who are inferior to him in these qualities. As the supreme excellence is, by subjection of the passions, to attain to the extinguishment of desire ; and as the continuing in secular employment and married life shows that the sensual principle is powerful, and that the desires of pleasure, gain, and ambition are in active operation, laymen are not the proper objects of this respect."

" No man can become an ordained priest unless he be, at least, twenty years of age, and has the permission of his parents, if they be living ; but he may leave the priesthood whenever he pleases, without any impediment to his returning to it when he finds it convenient."

"When a man assumes the yellow robe and becomes a priest, he solemnly declares that it is for the purpose of entirely subduing the principle of concupiscence, and of obtaining *Nirwana*, or freedom from continued existence." "Among themselves they are governed by seniority" in the priestly office; and the senior priest, although he may be the younger man, is entitled to the reverence of his fellows.

"The supremacy of wisdom and virtue being the governing principle of Buddhism," its adherents "regard with reverence the teachers of other religions, especially if their ceremonial does not require the taking of life. This will account for there being so much apathy among the Singhalese on the subject of Christianity, and for the facility with which they unite the worship of God with the adoration of Buddha and his priests. This does not appear to them to be a great violation of their system, if it be a violation of any kind. They acknowledge the Founder of Christianity to have been possessed of extensive wisdom and great benevolence; they consider him to have abstained from secular pursuits, and to have devoted himself to the instruction of men in wisdom and virtue; and that by his self-denial and labours for the good of others he exemplified his own operations. He is, therefore, a legitimate object of reverential adoration; but not to such an extent as Buddha, whom they regard as having been both wiser and holier than HE was, Buddha having discovered and taught the perfection of knowledge, especially that by which men may obtain *Nirwana*.

"The Singhalese have united demon-worship with Buddhism, and that frequently with bloody rites; but this is in direct opposition to the system. The demons are malignant, and therefore ought not to be worshipped; and if they have any power over men it is only in consequence of men's vices. The virtuous man may bid them defiance. But the tendency to this worship is so strong that the priests cannot check it;

and they submit to that which they cannot control, lest the people should withdraw from them. In the society of the intelligent they may speak of it as being incorrect, and endeavour to oppose it by recommending the ceremony called *Pirit*, or protection, which consists in reading a series of Buddha's discourses for a certain number of days without intermission, a sufficient number of priests being in attendance to continue it by day and night." " The people acknowledge the correctness of this doctrine, but under the influence of terror they still have recourse to demon ceremonies."

" Although the preceding exhibits the views of the learned and reflecting part of the Buddhist community, the great body of the people think little on the subject, and merely tread in the footsteps of their forefathers." " The teachings of Buddha do not sanction acts of immorality; but enforce justice, benevolence, and the social virtues." His system "requires a rigid course of virtue; and the consequences of evil conduct are represented as dreadful and ultimately certain." "He affirms that the sinner is miserable in this world, and will be so in that which is to come; and that there is no place in the earth, in the sky, or in a cave or rock, even to the extent of a hair's breadth, where the sinner can hide himself from the consequences of his crimes. The Buddhists of the present day do not deny this, but they avail themselves of other doctrines to render these practically useless." It is thus that "the practical working of Buddhism is essentially different from its system."

" Goutama"—the last of the Buddhas—" differed from those of the other Indian philosophers principally in two points, namely, the nature of transmigration, and *Nirwana*, or extinction of being. He affirmed also " the undue influence of caste;" and " that the true Brahmin is not the man born of any peculiar family, but the individual who lives virtuously. Caste, accordingly, is not recognised in his code for the priesthood. The highest and the lowest stand there on an equality, and the only dignity is connected with seniority; so that if a

man born of low caste, and with very inferior talents, should
be the senior priest, his high-caste and talented juniors must
salute him with the utmost reverence as their superior.

" The general mass of the Buddhists in Ceylon are not
orthodox in their views of transmigration, as they believe that
the same soul migrates into different bodies ; but this is contrary to the teachings of Buddha, and of this the learned
priests are fully aware, but they do not attempt to correct the
error, regarding the subject as too difficult to be understood
by the unlearned.   His doctrine is that of a series of exist-
ences, which he illustrates by the metaphors of a tree and of
a lamp.   A tree produces fruit, from which fruit another tree
is produced, and so the series continues : the last tree is not
the identical tree with the first, but it is a result ; so that if
the first tree had not been the last tree could not have existed.
Man is the tree, his conduct the fruit ; the vivifying energy of
the fruit is desire ; while this continues the series will proceed : the good or evil actions performed give the quality of
the fruit ; so that the existence springing from those actions
will be happy or miserable, as the quality of the fruit affects
the tree produced from it.   When desire is extinguished, the
vivifying power of the fruit ceases, and no tree springs from
it ; existence terminates.   According to this doctrine, the present body and soul of man never had a previous existence ;
but a previously existent being, under the influence of desire,
performed virtuous or vicious actions : and in consequence of
this, upon the death of that individual, a new body and soul
is produced.   The metaphor of the lamp is similar : one lamp
is lighted from another ; the two lamps are distinct, but the
one would not have been lighted had not the other existed.
The nature of *Nirwana*, or cessation of being, is obvious
from this ; it is not the destruction of an existent being,
but a cessation of existence.   The lamp burns out, and in consequence of the destruction of desire there is no lamp, neither
wick nor oil for the kindling of a new one ; the series, therefore,
terminates.   It is not an absorption into a superior being, as

the Brahmins teach; it is not a retreat to a place of eternal repose free from transmigration, called the 'Hall of Glory,' or any other name; it is not a violent destruction of being, but it is a complete and final cessation of existence. According to this, Buddha is no more; he is unexistent. His doctrines remain, and the remembrance of his virtues and excellences; the belief of the one and the reverence of the other are virtuous acts, but Buddha himself has ceased to be. The correctness of this statement is indubitable; every Buddhist priest will confirm it, and the errors into which some authors have fallen on the subject can only have resulted from their imperfect knowledge of the native language, and the nature of some of the metaphors used in explaining the doctrine of *Nirwana*, which might lead a superficial inquirer to suppose that *Nirwana* is a place of undisturbed repose.

"Goutama did not profess to be a lawgiver, except with respect to his priests. To the general body of mankind he was only a teacher. In this character he represents himself as standing at the entrance of various paths, and seeing distinctly everything connected with them; he warns men, saying, 'O man! enter not into that path; if you do, such and such evils will befall you.'"

The foregoing extracts, from the writings of an experienced Christian missionary of undoubted zeal and indefatigable research, sufficiently explain the nature of the Buddhist system, which he and his fellows have undertaken, with God's assistance, to subvert; and which the British Government, by the 5th Clause of its Convention with the Kandian Chiefs, on the 2nd of March, 1815, undertook to protect in the following words:—"The religion of Buddha, professed by the Chiefs and the inhabitants of these provinces, is declared inviolable; and its rites, ministers, and places of worship are to be maintained and protected."

It is not, however, to the Convention of 1815 that we are to confine our attention, as to the provisions which are binding on the British Government in respect to the Buddhist religion;

for, in 1817, the Kandians rose in rebellion against the sovereignty of the British Government, and by such rebellion abrogated the provisions of that Convention. We must, therefore, turn to the Proclamation issued by Governor Sir Robert Brownrigg, on his successful suppression of rebellion on the 21st of November, 1818, which contains the following clauses :—

Clause 2.—" The exercise of power by the Representative of His Britannic Majesty from the date of that Convention, the 2nd of March, 1815, till the hour that insurrections broke out in the month of October, 1817, was marked with the greatest mildness and forbearance towards all classes ; the strictest attention to the protection and maintenance of the rites, ministers, and places of worship of the religion of Buddha ; and a general deference to the opinions of the Chiefs, who were considered as the persons best able, from their rank and knowledge, to aid the Government in ensuring the happiness of the mass of its new subjects. In exacting either taxes or services for the State, an extraordinary and unprecedented laxity was allowed to take place, in order that the country might with more ease recover from the evil effects sustained by the contrary practice of the late King. In assessing punishment for offences, even where a plot to subvert the Government was proved, the spirit which always characterizes the British rule was strongly to be contrasted with the ancient and frequent recurrence of capital executions, preceded by the most cruel and barbarous tortures."

Clause 21.—" The Governor, desirous of showing the adherence of Government to its stipulations in favour of the religion of the people, exempts all lands which are now the property of Temples from all taxation whatever ; but, as certain inhabitants of those villages are liable to perform fixed gratuitous services also to the Crown, this obligation is to continue unaffected."

Clause 56.—" In all matters not provided for by this Proclamation, or other Proclamations heretofore promulgated by

the authority of the British Government, His Excellency
reserves to himself and to his successors the power of reform-
ing abuses, and making such provisions as are necessary,
beneficial, or desirable. He also reserves full power to alter
the present provisions, as may appear hereafter necessary and
expedient; and he requires, in His Majesty's name, all officers,
civil and military, all Adigars, Dissaves, and other chiefs, and
all other His Majesty's subjects, to be obedient, aiding and
assisting in the execution of these or other his orders, as they
shall answer the contrary at their peril."

In this Proclamation we find that the Temple lands are
exempted from taxation; but there is no express obligation to
uphold Buddhism: and even if there were, the reservations in
the 56th clause gives power to annul any, or all, of its previous
provisions.

It was for many years deemed politically inexpedient to
make use of the power reserved in the Proclamation, and give
over the custody of the captured Deladá, or relic of Buddha,
to the Kandian Chiefs and Priests; because the native tradition, that the security of the Government of the country
depended on its retaining possession of Buddha's tooth, continued to be as firmly believed by the Buddhists as it un-
doubtedly was in 1815 and in 1818, when it induced General
Brownrigg to yield to the representations of the Civil officers
in Kandy, and—regardless of the remonstrance of Sir Har-
dinge Giffard, the legal adviser of the Crown—to place a
guard of British soldiers over the relic, and promise *that* protection to Buddhism which has been the cause of so much
embarrassment to his successors, and which has led to such
diversity of opinions as to the best mode of relinquishing all
connection with idolatry.

In those days the Kandian country was encircled by dense
forests, through which our soldiers had to cut their way, often
in single file, with the greatest difficulty, exposed to deadly
diseases and festering leech bites. The loss of valuable lives,
great expenditure of money, and other serious disadvantages

P

under which the conquest had been achieved, induced those in authority to desire to secure peace and avoid the consequences of future rebellion.

The political exhibition of the Deladá relic, which took place in 1828, in the town of Kandy, was generally approved of at that time. Indeed, one of the oldest Missionaries in the Island was of opinion that, by publicly unveiling the super-stitious mystery which concealed the real nature of this imaginary tooth of Buddha in the presence of the Kandian people, the Governor had done more to sap the foundation of Buddhism than had been effected by missionary exertion. Other equally good men, who have subsequently commenced their Christian labours in Ceylon, have attributed to it a con-trary effect; but on such questions there will always exist some difference of opinion.

On the 1st of October, 1847, in pursuance of orders from the Secretary of State, the Deladá relic was given over by the Government into the charge of the Priests and Chiefs of the Kandian Province. To this act some persons have attributed the Kandian Rebellion in the succeeding year. It is probable that, like the impolitic attempt to impose a system of direct taxation on the people, it may have contributed to that un-happy result; but the germ from which the long-suppressed spirit of rebellion sprang was implanted in 1833—not so much by depriving the Chiefs and the Priests of the forced labour of their vassals, as by doing so without affording them any compensation whatever for their loss.

Soon after the rebellion of 1848 was subdued, the Priests of Buddha were specially exempted from the operation of the Road Ordinance, to which the English Clergy and all other Christian Ministers in common with all laymen, except the Governor and the soldiers, were subjected. This special men-tion of the Buddhist religion in a legislative enactment, has conferred a status upon Buddhism which it did not previously possess. This highly objectionable status cannot be too soon rendered innocuous by legally exempting *all* ministers and teachers of religion from the operation of the Road Ordinance, without special mention of any sect.

In a despatch, dated the 10th of May, 1819, addressed by Governor Viscount Torrington to the Secretary of State, and published in Ceylon, it appears that the act of handing over the custody of the Deladá relic to the Priests of Buddha, had not wholly severed the connexion between the British Government and the Temple authorities; that the rights of Kandian sovereignty, undertaken by the British, involved the duty of appointing succeeding Priests and lay-officers, called Basnaike-nillemes, to the occurring vacancies in the several Temples; and that, without such appointments under the Governor's signature, the rights of the Temples to the rents of their lands could not be enforced by law. Such being the case, a wrong existed irrespective of religious consideration: and, although it was desirable that the Governor should cease to issue written appointments, testifying to the "learning and piety" of the new incumbents, and refrain from any overt official act either to hasten or prevent the crumbling to pieces of mouldering monuments of idolatry,—nevertheless, property should be protected by the law of the land, no matter to whom belonging. Besides, the Kandian people desired that the right of sovereignty over these Temple lands should be preserved; and who can tell how soon these Temple land-rents may become —equally by the desire of the people—an additional means of extending Christian instruction among their children. That such is likely to be the case in the Kandian Province, is the belief of one of the oldest residents both in it and in the maritime districts.

In order to enforce the rights of property and insure the due collection of rents from tenants of Temple lands, and thus while exercising the rights of sovereignty also to perform its duties, it was considered that, on the decease of the Temple incumbents, whenever the tenants withheld their rents the estates might be administered by the official administrators of the respective District Courts, who could collect the rents, and

deposit them with the Loan Board, subject to the orders of
the Governor to pay them over to the persons in peaceable
possession of the respective Temples to which the estates
belonged,—even as other intestate estates are liable to be
administered, and the funds deposited with the Loan Board,
subject to the orders of the Supreme Court,—or, that the Governor should grant the persons in peaceable possession of the
respective Temples such certificates as would enable them to
enforce their claims to the rents of the Temple lands in the
District Courts, without any allusion whatever to religion;
and this latter proceeding, it appears, has been successfully
adopted.

CASTE.—The serious evils and inconveniences occasioned by
the prejudices of Caste in Hindostan, are scarcely felt in
Ceylon, for there the Mahomedans are so generally engaged
in trading pursuits that very few of them enter indoor domestic service; and the few Hindoos who do so—although
strict in outward adherence to their caste—appear to be fully
aware that it is not in the power of other men to deprive
them of it; for while both Mahomedans and Hindoos indig-
nantly resent any defilement from forcible contact with such
substances as they deem to be unclean, they nevertheless
hasten to wash and be clean. As caste forms no part of the
system of Buddha, the Singhalese have no apprehension of
losing it. With them caste appears to be the result of some
early arrangement for insuring a division of labour which has
long since been unheeded; and is not this the case with our
London guilds? As in London a freeman of the Goldsmith's
Company may be a tailor, so in Ceylon a Vellala of the highest
caste may be a domestic servant, with the only advantage of
being acknowledged by his fellow-servants to be of higher
caste than themselves.

The learned Mahomedans and Hindoos of Bengal know full
well that religion is of the heart, and that the convictions of
the heart cannot be affected by any accidental, or forcible,

contact of their flesh with unclean substances; but they are induced by their worldly interests to cherish in their ignorant fellow-countrymen that erroneous belief in the connexion between religion and caste, which has been so craftily inculcated by their priests, and to foster the absurd apprehension that the using of greased cartridges would deprive them of their religion. Such delusions are fast dying out among the Ceylonese; and it is to be regretted that the Christian zeal and energy which is now being expended in vain attempts to abolish caste in Hindostan, could not be concentrated on the severance of the connexion between it and religion in the unlearned Hindoo mind. Caste, unconnected with religion, is powerful in all societies and among all peoples. It is strongly implanted in Europeans; it exists nowhere with greater exclusiveness than in the Indian Civil Service; and our churches are partitioned into pews, as it were, for the purpose of preserving it among ourselves: * but as it is so

---

* Distinction in rank, and grades in society, must ever remain; but whenever the prejudices of caste are indulged to the detriment of the public, they should be removed. Our present volunteer movement is generally held to be a great success, so far as the defensive land forces of the nation are concerned; but this cannot be said of any voluntary movement among the mariners of England, for the volunteers of the Royal Naval Reserve, unlike those in aid of our land forces, are paid for their services. Our land volunteers are not liable to be employed in aggressive war, for they volunteer to serve in their embodied state under the immediate command of their own officers in defence of our soil from hostile invasion; their motto is "Defence, not Defiance." The volunteers of the Naval Reserve, being paid for their services, may be drafted to complete the crews of the ships in H.M. fleet, and employed in aggressive war—their motto being in effect both "Defence and Defiance." Both these voluntary forces—one paid, and the other unpaid—promise to be successfully kept up, and both are excellent for the purposes for which they are raised. But why have we not *unpaid* naval volunteers? Why should not the officers of the noble ships of our commercial marine be induced, without payment from the State, to study naval gunnery, and teach it to their respective crews? In war time their own interest would be, as in former wars, sufficient inducement; but in peace they have no such immediate interest to incite them, and therefore some such interest needs to be held out by the nation. If attempted to be enforced on them

closely and so injuriously connected with the religion of the
natives of Hindostan, it is the duty of Europeans, by Christian
example and the diffusion of education, to endeavour to sever
this absurd connexion, which so enslaves the people, and
which brought on them the sad consequences of the Sepoy
mutiny in 1857.

MISSIONARY LABOURS. — The Ceylonese are, beyond all
doubt, very much indebted to Christian Missionaries. A
great many of the active members of the present generation received their English education in Mission schools,
and owe to them their instruction in the truths of Christianity. The Singhalese, who form the largest portion of
the inhabitants, may be considered as an inoffensive, or-
derly race. · Many of the uneducated among them continue
the worship of demons, notwithstanding such practice is contrary to the teachings of Buddha, who taught his followers to
reverence virtue and wisdom; but as he did not instruct them
to trust in a Creator, it is extremely difficult to kindle gratitude and love towards Almighty God in hearts superstitiously
devoted to the cowardly worship of the devil; nevertheless,
there are many good Christians among the poor Singhalese.
There are several educated Singhalese and Tamil gentlemen
in holy orders; and many others are teachers of the Gospel
under the direction of European Missionaries. It has been
observed, with much satisfaction, that Christianity has advanced at an increased rate since the establishment of the See
of Colombo. Several handsome churches have been erected
at the principal stations; and many smaller ones in the in-

---

by Act of Parliament, it would be opposed to the voluntary principle
and would not succeed. The officers of our unpaid land volunteers have,
for the time being, honorary rank with those of the regular army. Why
should not similar temporary honorary rank be held out as an inducement to officers of unpaid sea volunteers? There is, no doubt, some
reason, and it may be a good one, if it does not spring from some undue
prejudice of caste existing in the Royal Navy.

terior of the Island, and in the villages around Colombo. It is not only the Church of England that has been invigorated by the Episcopate; but the impetus it received has no doubt had a beneficial influence on the work of all the other missions.* As the sea coasts of the Island were for upwards of 150 years in possession of the Portuguese, the Roman Catholics have many churches in the maritime provinces built and supported by the people, the fishermen being considerable contributors; and the Roman Catholics are now, as well as the Protestants, busily engaged in the conversion of the Kandians. But the Dutch, who succeeded the Portuguese, and held possession more than half a century, have comparatively but few Presbyterians remaining.

Sir James Emerson Tennent, in his valuable work on Ceylon, (vol. i., p. 379,) says, " the sentiments embodied in one of the edicts of King Asoca are very striking :—' A man must honour his own faith without blaming that of another, and thus will but little that is wrong occur. There are even circumstances under which the faith of others should be honoured; and in acting thus a man increases his own faith and injures that of others. Whoever he may be who honours his own faith and blames that of others out of devotion to his own, that man merely injures the faith he holds. Concord alone is to be desired.'" In these sentiments we have a key to the toleration evinced by the Buddhists, and the indifference with which their priests regard the labours of Christian Missionaries. The Buddhists of the district of Badulla have, by voluntary subscriptions, erected an Episcopal church in memory of their late able ruler, Major Rogers, of the Ceylon Rifle Regiment; and a Singhalese Chief has been

---

* At Moretto, about seven miles from Colombo, on the road to Point de Gallo, a handsome church has recently been constructed. The expense of its erection and the fund for its endowment being wholly provided by a munificent Singhalese gentleman, who, a few years since, was raised to the honorary native dignity of Modelier.

known to bequeath money towards the erection of a church as well as towards the support of a temple.

All the nations of the East, who are subject to English rule, desire that their sons should receive an English education, in order to facilitate their advancement in life. When a Kandian Chief was told by the Rev. Principal of an educational establishment in Colombo, that his son, on becoming a pupil, would have to attend Christian worship, he replied that religion was his son's own affair; that he himself believed Christianity was as good a balance for Buddhism as an outrigger was for a canoe, to prevent its upsetting. With all this apparent toleration of other creeds and desire for the education of their boys, but few adults forsake Buddhism and embrace Christianity. The desire of all Buddhists being to secure complete extinction of being, they do not fear death; nor can they value life in a future state. All their desire is to avert calamity in this world; and, as they know not God, when afflictions befal them, they direct their efforts to appease the enmity of the devil. Education is, therefore, the means mainly depended on for the spread of Christianity among the rising generation, particularly by its infusion through the medium of female schools. God grant that education may be more successful in converting the children of Buddhist parents, than it is said to have been among the Hindoos of Jaffnapatam. But the Hindoos and the Buddhists are very different people; and the method which is unsuccessful with the former may be successful with the latter.

The labours of Christian Missionaries have been attended with considerable success among the Islanders of the Pacific Ocean, where the communities are small, and where no deep-rooted system of false religion or philosophy, like that of Hindooism, previously prevailed. They have also been comparatively successful among the poor population of Southern India. But the highly learned Hindoos continue to resist the truth of Christianity, and baffle the efforts of good men devoted to effect their conversion. With the learned Hindoos lies the difficulty, which requires the most serious attention of Protestant England. To convince these learned Hindoos of the truths of Christianity, and upset their false system of philosophy, is a work worthy of the highest intellect and learning of the age; for it is evident that their cunning is proof against the ability of those good men of various Christian sects who have hitherto had to assail their errors. It is, however, very much to be feared, that the mere sending forth to India of the brightest intellect among our learned divines and profound theologians would not be sufficient, unless all Missionaries and teachers of Christianity in that country would hold them up to the natives as leaders in the great work of preaching the Gospel to all men. But, divided as we are into so many sects, is that union of purpose which is necessary to produce such general acknowledgment to be expected? If not, then what is to be done to christianize the learned Hindoos without reference to their being converted to any particular sect? We cannot abandon the field to the Roman Catholic Mission, nor aid it with our funds. It is possible that Roman Catholic unity of action, aided by our funds, might be attended with better success; but then, in proportion to that success, Roman Catholicism would become the religion of our Eastern Empire. We should remember that these learned Hindoos, who believe that consistency of practice is the best test of truth, are fully aware that the Church of England, to which the clergy paid by the Government belong, professes to be a branch of the primitive Church originally planted by the Apostles; that Romanists and Ultra-Protestants dissent, some from its creeds and doctrines, and others from its government and connexion with the State; that they also notice that each Christian sect, while striving to convert the heathen, is also as eager to make proselytes from other Christians in order to swell the number and increase the importance of their own respective folds; and that they conclude, in consequence of these differences and rivalries, that while all may be contending for that which they believe to be truth, it is quite impossible that all can be right, and that it is possible that all may be wrong. Also, that when they see English clergymen attend the chapels and prayer-meetings of Protestant Dissenters, while dissenting ministers do not attend the services of the Church, and that Roman Catholics consistently avoid both and adhere closely to their own, they conclude — notwithstanding their deference to the wisdom of Governments—that England must be in error in establishing the creed of the least practically consistent of the several Christian sects as the religion of the State.

My attention was drawn to the consideration of the subject of Hindoo conversion by hearing of the little progress it was making among the Hindoo population of Jaffnapatam, notwithstanding the indefatigable exertions of those excellent Missionaries supported by our American kinsmen, and those by our own countrymen; and from some information gained from a highly educated gentleman of the Hindoo race, who held an important public situation in Ceylon. We were sailing one moonlight evening on a smooth sea along the western shore of Calpentyn, on our way to Colombo, when I availed myself of an opportunity, in the course of conversation, to observe, that it appeared to me very surprising that any one possessing so much general information, such knowledge of the English language and of the contents of the Bible as he did, should continue an idolater. He immediately replied, " Sir, you have made the common mistake of English gentlemen; I am not an idolater. Our Hindoo sacred books forbid idolatry as much as your Bible does." I observed, that I was very glad to have this information; but, I asked, " Did you not subscribe largely to the funds for building the Hindoo Temple, in Sea-street, in which idols are placed and worshipped by the people?" He replied, "Yes, I did so; but you cannot suppose that I believe that those figures of wood and clay, made at my expense, can ever benefit me? Of course not." " But," I asked, " why do you, on entering that Temple, make your obeisance to those images as you pass them?" "Because," said he, "I should otherwise damage my position among my own people."

This wealthy Hindoo gentleman subsequently placed his only son under the tuition of the Reverend Chaplain of the Scotch Presbyterian Church; and it has been said that his preceptor entertained great hopes that the youthful mind of his intelligent pupil was impressed with the truths of the Gospel. But so far as outward appearances justify conclusion, since this well educated young gentleman has succeeded to the estates and wealth of his deceased parent, whose remains were burnt in accordance with Hindoo custom, he treads in the footsteps of his father as a high-caste Hindoo.

No doubt the mind of this young man was impressed with the kindness he received from his reverend preceptor and his truly excellent wife, and that he spoke of them to his father in affectionate terms, and of the good opinion he had imbibed of their religion. But this good opinion could be readily modified by his father's replying, that no doubt they were good people, and that the Bible was an excellent book; but that as Christians differed so much in its interpretation, and were so intolerant of each other's views, it was impossible they could be right; and that before Hindoos could place confidence in Christianity, its votaries must agree as to what Christianity is. We may thus perceive how it is that faith in Hindooism may be shaken without being supplanted by Christianity, and that these learned Hindoos place their sons under the instruction of Christian Missionaries for worldly advantage. Now, as we cannot abandon the Hindoo Missionary field to the Roman Catholics, could not religious England profit by the example of military England, bearing in mind that "the children of this world are wiser in their generation than the children of light?" With each arm of our military service, and each regiment acting as so many independent armies, acknowledging no Commander-in-Chief, is it to be supposed that the Bengal mutiny could have been suppressed? In military operations we saw that union, under one visible head, gave irresistible power to the whole army, and accomplished the end in view. We must not forget that this union was not merely apparent, but that it was real *bonâ fide* submission to the orders of one man. In dealing with the learned Hindoos every semblance of union will most assuredly fail. The mere semblance of union never did completely succeed with any men; but with them it is not only necessary to be sincere in all we attempt, but we must strive to be above suspicion of insincerity. Such being the case, and union of action under one visible head for the attainment of the conversion of the Hindoos being impossible; there appears to be but one alternative, founded on the Christian precept of brotherly love. We must cease to revile each other, subdue our mutual jealousies, and be strictly consistent in our proceedings; each sect steering by the principles of the Society to which it belongs—nothing wavering; and while steadily pursuing its course by the light it possesses, and glorying in the successful conversion of the Hindoos to its own Christian views, rejoice with equal thankfulness at the success of its allies in gaining converts to their respective folds. There should be no proselytizing from each other's flocks, nor sacrifice of principle, nor semblance of unity where real unity does not exist; but a declared acknowledgment of one common object by independent action—the winning of souls to Christ.

Now that India has become subject to the direct government of the Crown, it is highly probable that Europeans will visit it in greater numbers than heretofore. It is, therefore, of the very first importance, that all who do so, particularly those who take up their residence there, should be fully impressed with their responsibility as the representatives of Christian England in Hindostan. It is evidently the design of Providence that the English should be the pioneers of Christianity to the heathen world; and for this purpose, and not on account of their own deservings, the Empire of the East and other vast dominions have become subject to the British Crown. It is not expected that English merchants and planters should undertake the special work of preachers of the Gospel; far less is it desirable that officers, either civil or military, should do so in India; for there the very appearance of holding out any worldly advantage as an inducement to the subject Hindoo to become Christian should be carefully avoided : but all should let their Christian light shine before men, and by their example endeavour to impress the natives with kindly feelings towards them, and to create in them a desire to become acquainted with that faith which springs from gratitude to God, and leads to love and goodwill towards all men !

PART II.

OBSERVATIONS

ON

SIR JAMES EMERSON TENNENT'S "ACCOUNT OF CEYLON."

OBSERVATIONS

ON SIR JAMES EMERSON TENNENT'S "REASONS FOR
BELIEVING THAT THE SITE OF TARSHISH MAY BE
RECOGNISED IN THE MODERN POINT DE GALLE."—
Vol. i., p. 530.

-

AFTER the indefatigable researches of Sir James Emerson
Tennent into the ancient accounts of Ceylon, it would ill
become one, who has not the least pretensions to literary
acquirements or learned research, to regard the opinions of so
accomplished a writer otherwise than with the greatest deference and respect. It is, therefore, with considerable re-
luctance that I venture, in my uncultivated style, to oppose my
conclusions, founded on professional experience, to the infe-
rences he has drawn respecting the port of Point de Galle having been "the centre of the more important commerce between
China and the West,"* and that it may be recognised as the
site of that ancient emporium of commerce from whence " the
fleets of Solomon were returning, when once in every three
years came the ships of Tarshish, bringing gold and silver,
ivory, apes, and peacocks." †

Sir James Emerson Tennent does no more than infer from
his researches the reasonableness of the conjecture of others—
" that it may possibly have been Ceylon, and certainly from
southern India"—that Solomon obtained his precious triennial
supplies. I am by no means competent to question the sound-

* See Sir James Emerson Tennent's " Account of Ceylon," vol. i.,
part v., chap. ii., p. 565.
† See vol. i., part v., chap. i., p. 530—foot note.

ness of this inference, or to offer an opinion as to the country from whence the ships of Tarshish * obtained their lading. I must leave that question to be settled by those learned men who have made the subject their study. My object, I might almost say my duty, when I consider what was my professional position in Ceylon, is to show that, *if* the ships of Solomon reached that Island *every three years*, they may have frequented that harbour which is entered at Hippuros, now called Koodremalle ; but that the obstacles presented by the monsoon winds and currents to such early navigators, B.C. 1,000, would have been too great to admit of *triennial* visits to the Harbour of Point de Galle.

In a pamphlet which I had printed at Colombo in 1835, under the signature of "Nota Bene," I ventured an opinion on the origin of the large tanks, embankments, and other ruins in the northern portion of Ceylon, which Sir James Emerson Tennent has so admirably described. I then suggested to my friends, that "the map of India should be spread before us, the prevailing monsoons be considered, and their effect on navigation in those ages when the north-western and the eastern portions of Ceylon were the marts for the exchange of merchandise between Arabia and China ; that the great influx of traders would render the supply of food extremely precarious in places subject to lengthened draughts, as these parts of Ceylon not unfrequently are ; and that, as the cost of freight in those days must have been far too great for the conveyance of grain by sea, it is reasonable to conclude that necessity suggested the construction of tanks for preserving the supply of water, which the wealth of an extensive trading population rendered practicable. Again, let the site of Anarajapoora be considered with reference to these tanks; also the excellent harbour for ancient shipping between

---

* May not "Tarshish" have been a general term for commerce, whether applied to emporiums of trade or to ships engaged in commercial pursuits ?—See 1 Kings, chap. xxii., 50.

Koodremallo and the Isles of Calpentyn ;* also the site of the ruins of Mantotte, so near to these decayed tanks, and the shelter afforded by the Island of Manaar, and it will require no great stretch of imagination to trace the origin of both cities and tanks to the proximity of the seats of extensive commerce. But as the knowledge of navigation improved, and voyages round Ceylon were effected, these ancient marts necessarily began to decline, and their populations consisting chiefly of traders gradually followed the course of trade, until there were not sufficient inhabitants left to keep in repair the tanks and embankments then becoming, as they now are, unnecessary."

I find that the opinions of Bertolacci on this subject—referred to by Sir James Emerson Tennent—are so much more forcibly expressed, that I cannot refrain from making the following extract from the Introduction to his commercial work on Ceylon, published in 1817 :—

"It seems incontestable that Indian nations, not the Aborigines of Ceylon, had, from the most early times on record, taken possession of that portion of the Island, and expelled the Ceylonese, if these in truth did ever inhabit it. Commerce, however, and not the indulgence in a spirit of conquest, was, in my opinion, the pursuit of those nations.

"I suppose that, in remote antiquity, the coasting trade, from one half of Asia to the other half, must have passed through the Straits of Manaar ; and that, consequently, a great emporium was formed on the coast of Ceylon opposite to it.

"Prior to the discovery of the compass, when mariners could not safely venture from the sight of land, they had no alternative, in passing from the Malabar to the Coromandel coast, but by the Straits between Ceylon and the Peninsula,

---

* This harbour afforded shelter to a Roman tribute ship in the days of Claudius.—See Sir James Emerson Tennent's " Account of Ceylon," vol. i., p. 532.

or by rounding that island.   To effect the latter, however, by
keeping close to the island, is impracticable, except by wait-
ing for the changes of the regular monsoons.   The south-west,
that blows from April till September, and is favourable to
vessels going from Capo Comorin to Manaar, or the coast of
Ceylon near it, renders it impracticable to proceed thence to
the point Dondora Head.   The north-east, that prevails from
October to the month of February, would facilitate the passage
of these vessels from Manaar to Dondera Head; but there
they must wait again for the south-west, before they can proceed to Trincomalie, Point Pedro, and the coast of Coromandel.   Even now that navigation is much improved, the
Indian vessels that trade between Ceylon and the coast of
Coromandel effect only one voyage in the year, and wait for
the change of the regular monsoon to undertake their return;
but larger vessels, with the assistance of the compass, carry
on an extensive and animated commerce from the Gulfs of
Persia and Arabia to the rich provinces of Bengal and China,
without even stopping at Ceylon for refreshments, but leaving
it at a considerable distance, unless when passing with the
favourable monsoon.

"If, therefore, to round Ceylon, they were compelled in
former times to employ at least twelve months, it is but fair
to think that merchants with vessels of different burdens
would flock to the Straits of Manaar, or to those of Pomben,
and that those vessels which, from their size, could not pass
these shallow straits, would be unloaded, and the merchandise
either removed in boats to be transhipped into other vessels as
they arrived from the opposite coast of India, or be deposited
in stores to await an opportunity of obtaining the necessary
conveyance.

"These circumstances must, consequently, have assembled
a large concourse of trading people on the shores of those
straits, and on the country contiguous to them.

"Many merchants from Persia and Arabia, from Surat and
the Malabar coast, would prefer disposing of their goods at

those places of depôt, and returning home with their ships laden with the produce of Coromandel, and of the countries near or beyond the Ganges. Hence, numberless establishments must necessarily have been formed at and near Manaar, for the convenience of many trading nations.

"The productions of different climates and the manufactures of different regions must have been brought to those great places of general resort, for the purpose of consumption and exchange. Hence the cause of a great population near Mantotte and Aripo; hence the origin of an extensive cultivation round the Giant's Tank, and the formation of that surprising work.

"But the use of the compass having subsequently been discovered and navigation improved, the trading through the Straits of Manaar soon became less profitable, and more tedious than by a direct voyage passing at a distance from the land, and was therefore abandoned; from which followed the decay of the establishments made at Manaar or the coast of Ceylon opposite to it, and the consequent depopulation of that country.

"The following reflections will corroborate these opinions :—

"In the first place, if the island had been invaded by a warlike people, for the sake of acquiring territory and wealth, they would have extended their conquests, and fixed their residence in that beautiful, pleasant, and rich part of the country, which is by far most preferable in point of climate, and for its aptitude to produce the finest fruit of the soil—I mean those provinces which now form the districts of Chilow, Colombo, and Point de Galle. But we do not find either from history, tradition, or monuments, that those provinces were ever in the possession of any nation but the Ceylonese, except probably the Bedas, whom we consider the true Aborigines of Ceylon. It is natural that the Ceylonese, on the other hand, having a pleasant and plentiful country to inhabit, would not extend their population to the barren and uncongenial sandy plains in the neighbourhood of Aripo and Mantotte; neither

could they feel great jealousy in strangers fixing their residence in those abandoned plains. However, supposing they
had an inducement to settle in that country, what means could
they have of arriving at a populous and flourishing condition
in a soil which, even with the exertions of man, can produce
but little besides rice, unless they derived very ample resources from commerce? This nation, or nations, seem to
have confined themselves as much as possible to that part of
Ceylon nearest to the Straits of Manaar and the Gulf of Jaffnapatam; those being the places where the trading vessels
were obliged to touch, and wait the changes of the monsoons,
and where the greatest depôts of the Eastern trade were consequently established. It suffices to cast an attentive look
upon the chart of the Peninsula of India and Ceylon, and
consider the direction of the monsoons, to be convinced that
my conjectures have every appearance of being well grounded
in reason.

"By the improvements which, in more modern times, have
been made in navigation, we have a satisfactory means of
accounting for the decay and desertion of that country, the
opulence of which was entirely dependent on commerce; and
we also find there a sufficient reason for the wars which,
it is reported, were undertaken by the Ceylonese kings
against the Hindoos established near Mantotte and Aripo,
and which terminated in a total subjugation of their
power, and the desolation of the country, which was, in
the end, deserted by the conquered as well as by the
victors.

"When these mercantile establishments began to lose part
of their strength and population, it is likely that the Ceylonese, feeling then their comparative superiority in numbers
and power, attacked the remnants of those establishments
with a view to pillage and rapine; and afterwards, when they
had fully obtained their object, withdrew to their pleasanter
climate and richer soil.

"The inscriptions which have been found in that part of

the coast (both on stones and on some gold coins excavated some time ago), in a language at present unknown, belong, probably, to some of the various trading nations, who had fixed their residence there and afterwards entirely abandoned it.

"We may also imagine, that the vicinity of the Pearl fishery to Aripo and Manaar may have added to the inducements of trading nations to fix their attention upon that part of Ceylon, although not in itself sufficient to have tempted them to establish a permanent residence in so barren a country."

Such were the opinions of Bertolacci in 1817, after sixteen years public service in Ceylon. I would now, in 1861, request those persons who may be interested in the Cinnamon Isle, to spare a little consideration to this not uninteresting subject, and spread before them a chart of the Indian Ocean—an advantage which the mariners of King Solomon's days did not possess. At the same time, it will be well to bear in mind the description of native craft in use in India and China at the present day, and reflect on the centuries that have elapsed since the ships "built by Solomon at Ezion-Geber, on the shores of the Red Sea," rowed "along the shores of Arabia and the Persian Gulf headed by an east wind," [*] and on the improvement that must have taken place—even in Indian craft—since that time. It is, I repeat, necessary that all these matters, as well as the effect of the monsoons, should be deliberately considered before an opinion is given upon a subject so interesting to many persons, although of no practical importance.

As these observations may meet with attention from persons who are not well acquainted with the effect of monsoon winds and ocean currents, I venture to offer some brief explanation of their nature and effect in the vicinity of Ceylon.

---

[*] See *Edinburgh Review*, No. 224 ; October, 1859, p. 345.

The Indian monsoons, or seasons, when spoken of by seamen, are misunderstood as applying to the prevailing winds
during the seasons of the year; and in Ceylon it is usual to
consider the year as divided into two monsoons,—the North-
east and the South-west. There are, however, intervals between these monsoons, in which calms and variable winds
prevail; and during these intervals the northern part of the
Island has sometimes been reached by the southern margin of
cyclones from the Bay of Bengal. It is sufficient for the
purpose in view to confine these observations to the effect of
the monsoon winds in producing that motion in the waters of
the ocean, known as currents, rather than to enter upon the
consideration of the causes of the monsoons. We know that
each monsoon prevails, with more or less force and with few
short intervals, for one-half the year. We see on the chart,
that the continent of Hindostan extends to the southward of
eight degrees of latitude, and that the Island of Ceylon, which
is partially connected to it by Adam's Bridge, extends still
further southward across the course of these monsoons; and
we perceive that this extension must obstruct the natural
courses of the currents caused by them. We know that where-
ever a stream is obstructed in its course that some slight reaction takes place; and that wherever the obstructed stream
finds an escape, it is there that its force is increased in proportion to the obstruction it has met with in its natural course.
Such is the case with the ocean currents, where they escape
round the southern coast of Ceylon; and wherever the line
of that coast presents the most abrupt turning, as it does about
Point de Galle, we find not only the greatest force of the currents, but the greatest uncertainty in that force, and sometimes variation in their direction, even to the extent of
counter currents, or eddies of short duration, like the lulls in
the monsoon winds which occasion them.

Now, if we refer to the chart, and suppose the north-east
monsoon to be at its height, which is the case in the month of
January, we have a strong wind blowing the waters of the

Bay of Bengal towards the south-west. But as the natural direction of this south-western current is impeded by the coast of Coromandel and the east coast of Ceylon, it becomes impelled towards the south along these coasts with increasing force until it escapes round the southern part of Ceylon, and then resumes its course with the wind. The same north-east wind prevails with even greater force in the Gulf of Manaar; but its effect is not to depress the level of the sea on the north-eastern shores of that Gulf, as might be supposed: for it is then preserved at its maximum height by an influx round Point de Galle, which commences as the south-western monsoon abates, and causes a northerly current to flow past Colombo in October and November, which continues to be slightly felt during the strength of the north-eastern monsoon, and assists vessels in beating up the western coast. There is also a portion of the water from the Bay of Bengal driven into Palk's Gulf, which raises the surface on the northern side of Adam's Bridge sufficiently to reopen the scours closed by the sand forced up by the violence of the south-western monsoon, and this flow through the reopened scours and the navigable channel at Paumben causes a current to set to the southward along the coast of Madura, and must necessarily assist in raising the level of the sea on that coast. Ships leaving Bombay in the height of the north-east monsoon to load cotton at Tuticoreen, after passing Cape Comorin, find the southern current so strong as to induce them to stretch across the Gulf of Manaar and beat up the western coast of Ceylon until they can steer for their destined port, and this they accomplish against what is called in Ceylon the "along shore wind." This "along shore wind," while it lasts, blows with considerable force; for as it moderates so does it vary in its direction until it becomes land and sea breezes and ceases to blow "along shore."

March is generally a calm month in the Indian seas. It is the season of land and sea breezes, when the Pearl fisheries are held in the Gulf of Manaar. In April the wind is variable;

s

but sometimes the south-west wind blows fresh for several days, and is the commencement of the south-west monsoon; but this monsoon more frequently sets in early in May.

On referring to the chart we perceive that, as the north-east monsoon blew the waters out of the Bay of Bengal, so the south-west monsoon must blow them into it, and raise, or restore, the level of the sea on the northern and eastern shores. Even so it might be supposed to blow the water from the south-west into the Gulf of Manaar, and raise its level on the southern shore of Manaar and the western coast of Ceylon; but such is not its effect, and this peculiarity has to be accounted for.

As the strong south-west wind forces the water to flow towards the Bay of Bengal it depresses its level in Palk's Gulf, and the northern flat sandy shore of Manaar becomes dry for some distance in consequence. Now, if the south-west monsoon forced the water to flow from the southward into the Gulf of Manaar, as in theory we should expect it to do, the check to its progress at Adam's Bridge would cause it to rise on the southern side of that barrier, and to rush through the several scours, or channels, to restore the level of the water in Palk's Gulf. I am aware that, at the commencement of the south-west wind in April, the water does run with force through these channels, particularly those near to Hindostan; but when the south-west monsoon has set in, the high sea that it causes in the Gulf of Manaar beats up the sand with such force as to choak up all channels and rivers' mouths exposed to it: nevertheless, the water thus obstructed by Adam's Bridge and Manaar, in what would appear to be its natural course, does not rise, and the level of the sea on the western coast of Ceylon, from Manaar to Colombo, is then at its minimum height. Therefore, instead of the obstruction at Adam's Bridge and Manaar causing the water to rise on their southern sides in the south-west monsoon, it appears to have the contrary effect; and in the absence of a free passage between Hindostan and Ceylon the ocean current not only wholly sets past the southern shore of the latter, but draws the water from the Gulf of Manaar and depresses it at Colombo to its minimum level ; and it is found that ships leaving Colombo in the height of the south-west monsoon, are assisted out of the Gulf by a slight current setting to the southward along the western coast.

In alluding to currents within the Gulf of Manaar, it may be necessary to state that, except it be at the close of the south-west monsoon when the level of the sea is being restored by an influx from the southward round Point de Galle, the currents on the Ceylon side of the gulf are of such little force as never to occasion inconvenience.

In these days we are so much accustomed to the facilities of steam navigation, that the difficulties and delays experienced by sailing vessels in contending with Indian monsoons and currents are apt to be overlooked, and therefore a few instances for the elucidation of the object in view may not be amiss. Firstly :—As regards the currents on the eastern coasts of Hindostan and Ceylon. The ship *Eclipse*, from Calcutta, sighted Madras on the morning of the 11th of November, 1819, and the passengers prepared to land, but the wind failed before anchorage could be reached. With the buildings of the town distinctly in view, the becalmed ship was carried past the port by the strong southerly current, and she did not reach the anchorage until the 18th. Similar delay has been experienced by two of our Admirals bound for Trincomalie—off which port there is no anchorage—and it was by no means an unfrequent occurrence. Secondly :—As regards the winds. In January, 1818, the *Leda* overtook between Point de Galle and Colombo the Portuguese ship, which in those days brought the annual supplies from China. This ship was five days beating from Point de Galle against the northerly wind, and most of that time under double-reefed topsails. I have since known merchant ships to have been five times as long in accomplishing the same passage in the south-west monsoon, and to have been six weeks between

Trincomalie and Colombo at the same season of the year; for when the south-west wind is at its greatest strength off Point de Galle and along the southern coast, it takes the direction of the shore, and forces sailing ships to make what is called the southern passage, which takes them sometimes near to the equator. Native craft cannot contend against such strong winds, nor can they attempt a southern passage. When ships bound for Point de Galle in the south-west monsoon have missed the port and fallen to leeward of it, they have been several weeks in reaching it. Small brigs and schooners so circumstanced do not attempt to contend with the monsoon wind, but sail round the Island, pass through the channel at Paumben, beat along the Madura shore towards Cape Comorin, and from thence cross the Gulf of Manaar, in order to gain their destined port. I therefore cannot believe that, if ever the ships of King Solomon reached the shores of Ceylon, they ventured to steer for Point de Galle. It is true that, towards the close of the south-west monsoon, the Singhalese Dhonies proceed to sea and sail for Madras, and the Maldivian mariners leave their island attols for Ceylon and Bengal. It is also true that, during the north-east monsoon, such native craft trade on the western coast of India from Ceylon to Bombay; but they are well acquainted with the seasons, and keep near to the shore, availing themselves of the land and sea breezes on the Malabar coast, where they are more regular than on the coast of Ceylon, exposed, as the latter is, to the strong winds which prevail in the Gulf of Manaar. Nevertheless, these native vessels are sometimes caught by, and suffer from, the strong wind and high sea in the Gulf of Manaar.

Hitherto these observations may be considered as applying to the general effects of the monsoons on the coasts of Coromandel and Ceylon; but the exceptions to these general effects are not few, nor are they unimportant; for instance:—the strong south-west wind (which commences toward the end of April, or early in May, when the flow of water from the

southward has already commenced along the southern and
eastern coasts of Ceylon to restore its level in the Bay of
Bengal) drives the current on with such accelerated force, that
the maximum height in the bay is attained long before the
south-west wind has ceased, and, in consequence, a reactionary
current commences along its western shores. It is this reaction of the water towards the south that enables ships to
beat along shore from Calcutta to Madras in August and September; and, as the Bay of Bengal becomes surcharged with
water, the level of the sea on the shores of Jaffnapatam and
in Palk's Gulf is restored. It is at this period—which is
the driest season of the year—that the inhabitants of Jaffnapatam look for an increase of water in their wells, and
which timely increase they call the August flow. This increased supply of fresh water before any fall of rain has taken
place, is, beyond doubt, attributable to the rise in the level of
the sea and the percolation of its water beneath the fresh
water from the springs, checking its escape into the sea and
causing it to rise in the wells. But I shall have occasion to
revert to this subject before I close these observations.

Now, although there are brief intervals in the monsoons
when the wind moderates, particularly after the three first
months are passed, still these intervals are of short duration,
and are not to be depended on. Their effect, however, on the
current has sometimes been perplexing to navigators arriving
off the southern coast of Ceylon from distant places, particularly in the south-west monsoon, when, instead of the usual
strong easterly current, they meet with a westerly set as they
approach the land. These counter currents, like the lulls in
the monsoon winds which occasion them, are both uncertain
as to their duration and the time at which they may occur.
Similar uncertain refluxes take place in the north-east monsoon; but they are not attended with so much inconvenience.

The influence of the tide-wave is so little felt on the coast
of Ceylon, that it would be unnecessary to allude to it here,
were it not for the effect it has been supposed to have on the

quantity of water in some of the wells, and on the growth of the cocoa-nut tree near the sea. It is true that, when the tide-wave acts in conjunction with the strong wind of the north-east monsoon, the difference between high and low water at Colombo has amounted to as much as two feet and ten inches. But during the full strength of the south-west monsoon there is commonly not more than from three to five inches rise and fall, and that minimum difference has been observed to take place four times, instead of twice, in twenty-four hours, which is the case, I believe, with the rise and fall of the tide at Poole, on the coast of Dorsetshire.

It may be seen on reference to the chart of Ceylon, that the vessels in use by the early Chinese merchants would have found shelter at Trincomalie, and in several other inlets and bays on the eastern coast, even to the desolate south-eastern quarter of the Island where ancient ruins are still found. Batticaloa would appear to have been a most convenient place for obtaining cinnamon, where, we are informed by Sir James Emerson Tennent, it is now growing in sandy soil "in such quantity, as to suggest the idea that it must be the remains of former cultivation."* These early navigators would also have found shelter when needed by passing round the northern part of Jaffnapatam into Palk's Gulf, and there, near to Mantotte and Manaar, they would have had intercourse with the merchants of Arabia and Persia, whose vessels were sheltered at Manaar. Besides the shelter afforded at Manaar, it will be seen that within eight leagues to the southward of it there is, for such primitive craft, the best harbour in Ceylon, extending from Koodremalee to the southward of Putlam. We are informed by Sir James Emerson Tennent,† that a Roman tribute ship, in the days of Claudius, "having been caught by the monsoon was carried to Hippuros, the modern Koodra-

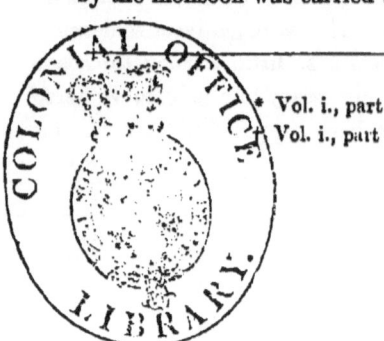

* Vol. i., part v., chap. ii., p. 578.

† Vol. i., part v., chap. i., p. 532.

mali, in the north-west of Coylon, near the Pearl banks of
Manaar. Here the officer in command was courteously received by the King, who, struck with admiration of the
Romans, and eager to form an alliance with them, despatched
an embassy to Italy, consisting of a Raja and suite of three
persons." It will be seen on the chart that the landing place
at Pomparipo in the port which is entered at Hippuros, is
the nearest part of the coast to the kingly residence at
Anuradhapoora.

It may be thought that the ships from Ezion-geber, in the
days of Solomon, might have been caught by the monsoon and
carried to Point de Gallo, even as the Roman tribute ship was
carried to Hippuros. This is possible, but by no means probable. The Romans, in their improved ships and their increased knowledge of navigation,* would venture much
further from the land than the merchant mariners of Ezion-
geber, who depended on their oars for advancing when the
wind was unfavourable. But if such an improbable accident
had befallen them, and they had been able to return home by
availing themselves of the season in which native Dhonies of
the present day (who do not use oars) make their passages to
Bombay, I am clearly of opinion that their visit to Point de
Gallo would not have been *repeated*, and we are told in Holy
Writ† that Solomon's navy came "once in three years."
This fact, when the description of craft and the difficulties of
the monsoons and currents opposed to them are considered,
appears to be quite conclusive that Point de Gallo was not the
commercial emporium of their day, nor are there any ancient
ruins in its neighbourhood to support an opposite opinion.

At page 312 of the first volume of his valuable "Account of
Coylon," Sir James Emerson Tennent pays a just tribute to the
estimable character and great ability of the late Honourable

---

* See Sir James Emerson Tennent, vol. i., pp. 530 and 531.

† 1 Kings, chap. x., 22.

George Turnour of the Ceylon Civil Service, the learned translator of the Mahawanso. From this translation of "the most authentic history of Ceylon," we learn that Wijayo, from Bengal, invaded the Island, B.C. 543, and that he fixed his capital at Tamana-Nuwera, which Sir James Emerson Tennent has placed on his ancient map, about ten miles E. by N. of Putlam—a town on the shore of the harbour which is entered at Hippuros, and which afforded shelter to the Roman tribute ship in the reign of Claudius.

In Sir James Emerson Tennent's "Account of Ceylon as known to the Phœnicians," (vol. i., p. 550,) the anchorage of the Tyrians is thus described:—"The roadstead was in front of a level strand, bordered with lofty trees, and coming on to blow at night, they were in the utmost danger till sunrise; but running then to the south, they came in sight of a safe harbour, and saw many populous towns inland." This remarkable description applies with singular fidelity to the strand of Manaar, with its lofty Palmyra trees; and "the safe harbour" "to the south" is equally as applicable to that which is entered at Hippuros.

Sir James Emerson Tennent also informs us (vol. i., pp. 335 and 587,) that the Chinese historian "Fa Hian states, that even before the advent of Buddha Ceylon was the resort of merchants, who repaired there to exchange their commodities for gems, which the 'demons' and 'serpents,' who never appeared in person, deposited on the shore, with a specified value attached to each; and in lieu of them the strangers substituted certain indicated articles, and took their departure." He also informs us, at page 335, that this story of Fa Hian "applies to the still existing habits of the veddahs;"* and at page 370, that "throughout the Singhalese chronicles the notices of the aborigines are but casual, and occasionally con-

---

* The veddahs of the present day deposit the produce they have to barter and retire, trusting to the honour of the stranger who removes it to leave in its stead articles known to be useful to them.

temptuous; sometimes they allude to ' slaves of the Yakko tribe;' and in recording the progress and completion of the tanks and other stupendous works, the *Mahawanso* and the *Rajaratnacari*, in order to indicate the inferiority of the natives to their masters, speak of their conjoint labours as that of ' men and snakes,' and ' men and demons.' "

We are further informed by Sir James Emerson Tennent, (vol. i., p. 394,) that the Malabars, or Tamils, " were natives of places in India remote from that now known as Malabar. They were, in reality, the inhabitants of one of the earliest States organized in Southern India, the kingdom of Pandya, whose sovereigns, from their intelligence and their managen ment of native literature, have been appropriately styled the ' Ptolemies of India ;' " that Wijayo, the Bengal conqueror, B.C. 543, " was connected by maternal descent to the King of Kalinga;" that "his wife was the daughter of the King of Pandya," and that the north-western portion of Ceylon was continually subject to invasions by Malabar adventurers. Again, at page 587 of the same volume, this indefatigable inquirer informs us, that " the Chinese were aware of two separate races, one occupying the northern and the other the southern extremity of the island, and were struck with the resemblance of the Tamils to the Hoo, a people of Central Asia, and the Singhalese to the Leaou, a mountain tribe of Western China."

Now, if we are to believe the statement of the Chinese historian, Fa Hian, page 335, " that even before the advent of Buddha [B.C. 624] Ceylon was the resort of merchants;" why should we not conclude that the temptation to plunder these merchants of their riches was as irresistible to the Malabars previous to the advent of Buddha as we are informed it was subsequently to that event; and that Wijayo—whether prince or robber, for he has been called both—was not the first invader of Ceylon, notwithstanding he may be the first recorded in the Mahawanso ? The late Sir Alexander Johnstone, in a note bearing reference to a map which ho propared to illus-

T

trate Captain Steuart's paper on the Pearl fisheries in 1833, alludes to "the account given by the *Hindús* of the several historical facts, upon which the Hindú poet, who composed the *Rámayana*, (a Sanscrit poem, said by the Hindús to have been composed many centuries before the Christian era,) founded the description which he gives of the conquest of the Island of Ceylon, the destruction of its tyrant Rávana, and the deliverance of Síta from her imprisonment on that Island by Ráma, whom he supposes to be the tenth incarnation of Vishnú : of the manner in which Ráma and his army crossed over the Gulf of Manár from the Peninsula of India to the Island of Ceylon, along the ridge of rocks known at present by the name of Adam's Bridge." *

From all these ancient traditionary accounts, and from the extraordinary researches of Sir James Emerson Tennent, we may not unreasonably conclude, that from the earliest period the northern portion of Ceylon was subject to frequent invasions ; not, however, as some have supposed, on account of the produce of its soil ; but from an irresistible desire on the part of the invaders to share in the riches of wealthy merchants assembled there from the east and from the west to barter, or exchange, the produce of their respective countries. No land subject to lengthened drought and failure of crops, with very few native inhabitants, and those few "living in the most primitive manner," would be, under ordinary circumstances, coveted by more civilized races from fertile lands, and yet it is in this most sterile part of Ceylon that such extensive ruins are found as are sure indications of considerable population in remote ages.

There exists some difference of opinion as to the landing-place in Ceylon of the Bengal invader Wijayo. Colonel Forbes is of opinion that it was at, or near Trincomalie : the Portuguese historian, De Conto, recording the Singhalese tra-

---

* "Transactions of the Royal Asiatic Society," vol. iii.

dition of the Portuguese, says he landed at Preaturo, between Trincomalie and Jaffnapatam; while Sir James Emerson Tennant informs us (vol. i., p. 330) that he "effected a landing with a handful of followers in the vicinity of the modern Putlam," which is on the eastern shore of the harbour which is entered at Hippuros. All, however, agree that his landing took place in the northern portion of the Island. On referring to the chart, we perceive that the considerable distance from Point Calymere to the nearest part of Ceylon—fully ten leagues—favours the opinion that a people so averse to venture on the sea as the Hindoos are known to be, would, like the invader Ráma, prefer the shorter course and smoother water near to Adam's Bridge, and endeavour to effect a landing at, or near to, the Island of Manaar. Now if this invader and his followers did land on the western side of Ceylon, I will venture to affirm that there is no part of the western coast so likely to have given rise to the "description in the Mahawanso of the landing of Wijayo,"* as that between Koodramalle and Putlam, more particularly near to the landing-place at Pomp-aripo, within the harbour which is entered at Hippuros, and which gave shelter to the Roman tribute ship in the days of Claudius. It is possible that Wijayo had not sufficient force with him to effect a landing at Mantotte or Manaar, where he might have been opposed by the traders, and that he proceeded southward, like the Tyrians, to the harbour at Hippuros, where he could effect his purpose. It may also have been the fewness of his followers which induced him to fix his residence so far south as Tamana-Nuwera instead of pushing on towards Anarajapoora, which is evidently the direction he desired to take, and that which 100 years later was taken by one of his successors, who established himself in that city. At this distant period, whatever may have been the case subsequently, it is evident that these

---

* Sir James Emerson Tennent, vol. i., part iii., p. 332.

invaders preferred the unproductive northern portion of Ceylon to its more fertile south; and it would appear that the
tanks they made were to provide for their own necessities, and
enable them to maintain their position in the vicinity of the
assembled foreign merchants whom they desired to plunder.
Ultimately, as these traders disappeared, the stream of immi-
gration appears to have taken a southerly direction, and the
Tamils, or, as they are frequently called, Malabars, were left
in permanent possession of the northern portion of the Island;
and their language is now spoken there " from Chilaw, on the
west coast, to Batticaloa on the east;" "whilst, to the southward, the vernacular is uniformly Singhalese." * In the most
remote parts of the interior there still exists a remnant of the
supposed aborigines—the veddahs—the "snakes and demons"
of the ancients; whilst on the shores of the harbour, which is
entered at Hippuros, the majority of the people are Moors,
the descendants of Arabian mariners, and excellent boatmen
they are.

We are informed in the Mahawanso that "Gotama," the
last of the Buddhas, was born B.C. 624; and that before his
birth Ceylon had been resorted to by foreign merchants. We
learn from Holy Writ that, B.C. 992, ships from Ezion-geber
were making voyages, once in three years, to some place
where they procured gold and silver, ivory, apes, and peacocks; and we are informed that the three last—ivory, apes,
and peacocks—are designated by the same names in the Hebrew and in the Tamil languages. † Surely this must be considered a remarkable circumstance in support of the opinion,
that these two peoples had early intercourse with each other,—
the latter being the inhabitants of the northern portion of
Ceylon. We find the description given by the ancient Tyrian
mariners of the strand off which they anchored to accord with

---

* Sir James Emerson Tennent, vol. i., p. 415.
† See *Edinburgh Review* for October, 1859.

that of the southern strand of the Island of Manaar—the nearest land to Adam's Bridge; and we find that they proceeded to the south and found shelter in a harbour which corresponds with that entered at Koodramalle, in which it is said that Wijayo effected his hostile landing B.C. 543, and still further with that which became the refuge of the Roman tribute ship, when caught by the monsoon and driven from the Red Sea. Now, when all these circumstances are deliberately and dispassionately taken into consideration, is it to be supposed, that these Roman mariners,—"who had given a new direction to navigation;" had "altered the dimensions and build of their ships," and "had imparted so great an impulse to trade,"—sought shelter in the narrow harbour at "Hippuros;" that the mariners of King Solomon, so many centuries before, after rowing along the shores of Malabar, round Cape Cormorin by Adam's Bridge to Ceylon, would have passed by the safe anchorage at Manaar and the excellent harbour at "Hippuros," and have ventured to steer for Point de Galle,—a voyage avoided by all ancient mariners as most dangerous and uncertain,—and that they would have repeated such reckless daring *every three years?* I must say that I am clearly of opinion that they would not!

At page 575 of his first volume, Sir James Emerson Tennent expresses an opinion, that, as cinnamon is not mentioned as an indigenous production of Ceylon by authors who wrote previous to the close of the thirteenth century, some suspicion is cast "on the title of Ceylon to be designated *par excellence* the Cinnamon Isle." But it may be asked, do the more ancient writers make special mention of cardamons, nutmegs, pepper, or of any other indigenous aromatic of Ceylon? In those days these aromatics were not cultivated. All grew wild in the forests or jungles, and all, when spoken of, may have been included under the general denomination of spices. The same difference in quality which exists now in the wild productions of the forests, may have existed then; and as the more excellent quality of cinnamon became appreciated and brought into repute, it attracted the special notice of the writers of the thirteenth century.

Probably the earliest mention of cinnamon by name is by Solomon in Holy Writ (Prov. vii., 17.)—"I have perfumed my bed with myrrh, aloes, and cinnamon." Now, "it is remarkable that the name of cinnamon in Hebrew is the same as in English." * And "it is very remarkable, too, that the terms by which some," of the imports from Tarshish, "are designated in the Hebrew Scriptures, are identical with the Tamil names, by which they are called in Ceylon to the present day: thus *tukeyim*, which is rendered peacocks in our version, may be recognised in *tokei*, the modern name of these birds; *kapi*, apes, is the same in both languages; and the Sanskrit *ibha*, ivory, is identical with the Tamil *ibam*." † It would not be unreasonable to infer from these coincidences, that the Hebrews of old had intercourse with the Tamils of the northern province of Ceylon, and that they gave the Hebrew names to its peafowl and apes, and adopted the Sanskrit name for ivory from the Tamil Ceylonese. Now it so happens that these three—ivory (or elephants), apes, and peafowl—are more commonly seen together in the northern portion of Ceylon than in any other part of the island. At daybreak, in the dry season, I have seen them on the bed of the river at Aripo wending their way with numerous other wild animals, in search of water in the hollow parts of the sand. In those early days it would have been much easier to have conveyed cinnamon and gold ‡ from the adjoining provinces, than to have conveyed peacocks twice or thrice the distance to

---

* See Parkhurst's note on Prov. vii., 17.

† See *Edinburgh Review* for October, 1859, p. 345.

‡ We are informed by Modelier L. de Zoysa—translator to the Government—that the gold found in Ceylon is generally alloyed with silver, varying from a fraction to 72 per cent.; but when pure, its specific gravity is 19·25. This gentleman has found it recorded in an ancient Singhalese work, that there were at one time sixty-four silver and sixteen gold mines in Ceylon.

Point de Galle, where they do not abound. It may, I think, be asked, if Solomon did not obtain his cinnamon from Ceylon, from whence did he obtain it? But if we were to admit, which I do not, that cinnamon is not an indigenous plant of Ceylon, still, so long as Ceylon produces the very finest quality in the world, I think it is entitled to be considered *par excellence* the Cinnamon Isle! *

I am aware that doubts have been entertained as to the cocoa-nut palm being an indigenous production of Ceylon ; but persons who have visited the tropical isles of the Indian and Pacific Oceans, are not likely to entertain an opinion that the cocoa-nut tree is not an indigenous plant, if indigenous means that the original seed was not planted by man. On all these isles it flourishes, particularly on the low shores of those least affected by the tide-wave. It has been said in Ceylon, that it is owing to some peculiar property in the sea breeze that its shores are in most places so beautifully fringed with cocoa-nut palms. But it is well known "that the young plant of the cocoa-nut, like all other plants, requires protection from the saline moisture of the sea air. It is true, that when it has grown sufficiently for its young leaves to be above such saline influence, that it flourishes in a remarkable degree as compared with those on higher ground. But this is because the tree thrives best when its fibrous root reaches fresh water, and this it does more readily on the low sandy margin near the sea. Cocoa-nut trees grow well and bear fruit on pure sand, provided the numerous fibres of their roots reach fresh water." † I am by no means sure that one would not grow in

---

* It used to be said, that the fragrance of cinnamon extended so far from the coast of Ceylon, as to be the earliest indication to the mariner of his approach to land. But in truth the only time that the cinnamon plant emits odour is when it is in blossom, and then it is remarkable for its unpleasantness. Its seed so closely resembles an acorn, that I have known a person recently from England receive one as an acorn, saying it was much smaller than those of our own land.

† My Report to the Government of Ceylon, dated the 3rd of May, 1848.

fresh water, as a hyacinth does in a glass, if the tree could be supported, and the fresh water not permitted to reach above the fibres of its root; for the tree withers when its stem remains too long flooded, and probably a hyacinth would do the same if planted too deeply in water.   Cocoa-nut trees grow faster in richer soil, provided their roots are kept moist, for fresh water is indispensable for their profitable growth, no matter where planted.   On some parts of the coast of Ceylon the ground rises gradually from the sea shore.   In such elevated sandy places the depth of soil above the fresh-water level is too great for the fibres of the roots of the cocoa-nut trees to reach it, and therefore trees so planted will not produce fruit under eight or ten years; whilst those planted within 200 yards on lower ground, where their roots reach the fresh water, will bear fruit in five years.

The rise and fall of tide on the shores of Ceylon is so very little that the effect is scarcely perceptible on the wells, particularly on those not very close to the sea ; but the rise and fall in the level of the sea appears to have more sensible effect on the wells at Jaffnapatam, owing, it is supposed, to the greater facility for the sea water to percolate through the apertures in the bed of madrepore upon which that peninsula is said to rest.   Now, a little reflection on what takes place at Dover, and, in all probability at some other English towns built over sea shingle, will render more clear what takes place in Jaffnapatam, and throw some light on the phenomenon observed in the well at Potoor.

In the lower part of the town of Dover some of the inhabitants are inconvenienced during the extraordinary high tides by the sea water oozing through the shingle beneath the fresh water from the springs, and raising it until it flows into the cellars and lower kitchens of the houses.   While fresh water is on the floorings of the buildings, the pumps when set in motion throw up saline water, and this continues until the sea water recedes with the falling tide and the spring water falls to its usual level.

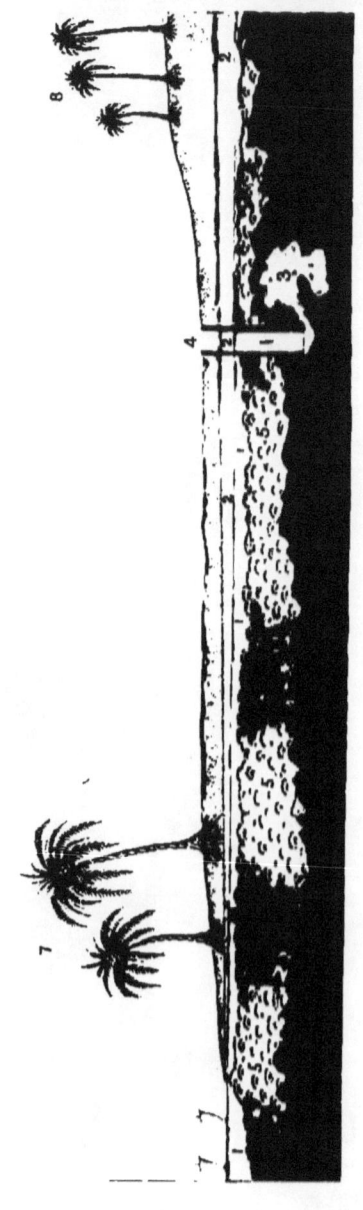

SECTION OF SEA COAST.

In the remarkable well at Potoor, the fresh water is not only supported by the sea water, but there is below both a fluid so exceedingly salt as to have been called brine, and, by those best acquainted with it, described as fetid. The existence of this stagnant water may be accounted for by the lower portion of the well communicating with some recess in the rock otherwise impervious to either air or water, and that this sole communication is by some small opening into the lower part of the well. But this conjecture may be better understood by an ideal representation of a section cut through the sea coast and passing through a supposed well, as shown in the diagram annexed.

REFERENCES TO DIAGRAM.

1. Sea water. 2. Fresh water. 3. Fetid water. 4. Well. 5. Porous madrepore. 6. Rock impervious to air. 7. Cocoa-nut trees with roots in fresh water. 8. Cocoa-nut trees on sandy bank, with their roots not in fresh water.

PART III.

A BRIEF NOTICE

OF THE

PEARL FISHERY

ON THE

COAST OF CEYLON.

THE Pearl fisheries in the Gulf of Manaar have always been regarded with great interest by the natives of southern India and of Ceylon. They have been held on banks lying off Tuticorin, in the territory of the Government of India, as well as on those near the shores of Ceylon from Chilaw to Manaar; but of late years the most productive Ceylon fisheries have taken place on the Aripo banks, between Koodremalle and Manaar, from eight to twelve miles off shore, in from four to nine fathoms water.

The great uncertainty which attends all that relates to Pearl fisheries increases the interest taken in them by the natives of the East, who delight in games of chance and speculation. There is not only the uncertainty as to the years in which they may take place; but when they do take place they last only a few weeks. They are as exciting to Indians as fairs, horse-races, and regattas are to Europeans; and much immorality attends them. But the revenue obtained from them is as great temptation to the Government as the gambling speculations are to the people, and experience has shown that casual revenue is as injurious to the former as gambling speculations are to the latter. After fisheries have been successfully held for several, nearly consecutive, years, the banks cease to be productive; and there have been very long intervals in which the disappointment has been very great, and not a little perplexing to the successors of those Governors of Ceylon, who, having had several successful Pearl fisheries, have caused the annual public expenditure to be increased, relying on the continuance of revenue from this most uncertain source.

Since I left Ceylon, the Government have engaged the

sevices of Dr. Kelaart, as Naturalist, to study the structure
and the habits of the pearl oyster. This gentleman's report,
dated at Trincomalie, in September, 1857, will no doubt be
interesting to the students of that part of natural history to
which it relates. He is of opinion, that pearl oysters may be
successfully translated to convenient localities, where they may
become a source of regular, instead of casual, revenue. If
this desirable result could be obtained, it would not only be
advantageous to the Government, but a great blessing to the
people who speculate at the fisheries; for then the price of
pearl would become less fluctuating, and the opportunities for
gambling speculations less frequent. Whether the present
value of pearl would be maintained with an abundant and
regular supply from such preserves, is quite another question.
It is, however, by no means certain, that if pearl oysters were
translated to preserved beds, they would produce pearl of
sufficient beauty and in sufficient quantity to pay the expenses
of such undertakings. There is not only a difference in the
colour and quality of pearl produced on different natural
banks, but in some places—of which Jaffnapatam is one—the
oysters do not contain pearl enough to pay the expenses of
their fishing; and, therefore, although the pearl oysters in such
artificial preserves might be as plump and as healthy as edible
ones on the Faversham beds, unless they contained sufficient
pearl of good quality they would neither be of value to the
State nor to the people.

It was not until I was preparing my account of the Pearl
fisheries for the Colombo press, in 1843, that I had access to
Mr. Lebeck's report of 1797, which I appended to my work.
In a note to his report, this gentleman writes, that "the depth
at which the pearl fish generally is to be found, hindered me
from paying any attention to the locomotive power, which I
have not the least doubt it possesses, using for this purpose
its tongue.* This conjecture is strengthened by the accurate

---

* Its foot, according to Dr. Kelaart.

observations made on mussels by the celebrated Reaumur, in which he found that this member serves them as a leg or arm to move from one place to another." To this he might have added, that the deck of a small vessel, with a comparatively numerous crew busily employed on the pearl banks, affords no convenience to a naturalist for watching the movements of captive animals so exceedingly sensitive as pearl oysters are said to be by Dr. Kelaart. But had Mr. Lebeck's opinion been known to those studious gentlemen in Ceylon, whom I repeatedly supplied with living specimens of the pearl oyster, which they dissected and preserved in the Colombo medical museum, it is possible that it might have led to a more early confirmation of the soundness of his conjecture; but the prevailing opinion in Ceylon on the power of loco-motion in the pearl oyster was as I described it in 1843. It was in November, 1851, that I accepted the public invita-tion of Mr. Hew Steuart, the editor of the *Ceylon Times*, to inspect, at his printing-office, some living pearl oysters which he had picked up on the sea beach during his morning walk, and which he kept in a glass globe filled with sea water; when, to my surprise, I saw that some of them had reached the surface of the water by extending themselves from out of their shells, and by creeping up the side of the globe— thus proving their power of locomotion when not attached by their byssus to immoveable substances. After this dis-covery, I took some glass globes to the pearl banks for the purpose of more attentive observation of the movements of the oyster; but those I placed in the globes exhibited no locomotive power, nor did they live long in confinement. The deck of a small vessel is not only unfavourable for such ob-servations, but the tropical heat on it is, no doubt, too great for animals taken from the cool recesses of the sea to live in, and it is thus that I account for the failure of my repeated attempts to convey live oysters from the pearl banks to Colombo before I resorted to floating perforated boxes, such as English fishermen use to convey living fish to market. It

remained for Dr. Kelaart, in his quiet retreat on the shore
of the harbour at Trincomalie, supplied with all the articles
enumerated by him as necessary for the performance of his
duties as Government naturalist, to discover that the pearl
oyster has the power of casting off its byssus from its own
body, of changing its situation, and of forming a new byssus
at its own pleasure.

PEARL FISHERY.

THE Pearl oyster of the Gulf of Manaar is not larger than the edible oyster of England; but unlike the edible oyster, its shells have a broad hinge, and the fish is supplied with a dark green fibrous byssus like that of a mussel, by the filaments of which it attaches itself to rocks, to the shells of its own species, or to any other substance. On account of these peculiarities naturalists have classed it with the mussel; but no fisherman would do so, nor would other persons who formed their judgment from the appearance of the shells, or from that of the fish within them.

The Pearl fishermen of Ceylon entertain a traditionary idea that pearl oysters descend with rain. This impression may be attributed to the well-ascertained fact, that in some parts of the East the spawn of fish has been drawn up and suspended in vapour until brought down by the rain, and such may have happened to the spat of pearl oysters. In the earliest stage of their existence they have been seen floating in immense quantities, as is the case with the spawn of other fish. While they are in this floating state they become attached to each other in clusters by means of their byssus; also to sea-weed, floating timber, buoys, cables, and even to the bottoms of boats when at anchor; and sometimes, after a strong wind has blown on the coast, large quantities are driven to the sea beach with the sea-weed and other floating substances to which they have adhered. Sometimes they are drifted by the force of the land wind, or carried by currents, to sink in a greater depth of water than divers can venture to explore. Some are devoured by other fish; and some, when from the ossification of their shells they have acquired sufficient gravity,

x

settle down upon ground unsuited for the production of pearl. It is, therefore, when they settle down upon, or subsequently find their way to, banks similar to those on which fisheries have been successfully held, that they produce pearl of sufficient value to be sought for. These favoured places appear to be sandy spaces interspersed with small spots of madrepore, to which the pearl oysters attach themselves and thrive. The depth of water over them varies from 4 to 9 fathoms; but the best fisheries have been in from 6 to 8 fathoms. Oysters, too young to contain pearl, have frequently been found on an extensive bank, which lies about six leagues from the land, in from 8 to 13 fathoms water; but the limited period that divers can remain under water would not admit of successful fishing in the latter depth, although some of the most expert have brought up such oysters as they found within their immediate grasp on reaching the bottom, and very small oysters have come up sticking to the tallow on the seaman's sounding lead.

Small pearls, or, as they are called, seed pearls, are sometimes found in oysters of four years old; but it is not prudent to hold a fishery before the fish has completed its sixth year. Seven years are considered by the fishermen to be the maximum age attained by the oysters, and the nearer they approach to that age the more valuable are their pearls. In the course of the seventh year the pearls increase in size so much as to double their value; and the temptation to benefit to the fullest extent by such increased value, has sometimes induced the postponement of a fishery until the oysters have died and the pearls have been lost.

It is believed that one hundred and fifty pearls—mostly small ones—have been found in one oyster. At the fishery of 1828 I counted sixty-seven taken from one of the oysters I obtained with those collected as my official privilege; but the greater number of oysters contain no pearl.

Pearls are supposed to be produced by some minute foreign particles getting in between the shells of the fish and exciting the secretion of the pearly matter which lines them. It is said to be the practice in some places to puncture the shells for the purpose of promoting such secretion. When pearls are cut into two parts they are seen to be formed in layers resembling those of an onion. They are found in all parts of the fish, and some are formed on the inner surface of the shells; these, being imperfect on the part next to the shells, are reserved for setting in gold. They are of various colours, some being black, while others are tinged a beautiful pink; but none are esteemed so highly as those of the prevailing silvery white, for the production of which the oysters from the Aripo banks are famous.

The immense quantities of pearl oyster-shells on the western sea shore of Ceylon are evidently the remains of very extensive fisheries in former ages. They are esteemed the best material for converting into that fine chunam which receives the beautiful polish so much admired in eastern buildings; but, being too thin for the general uses to which mother of pearl is applied in Europe, they have not hitherto been esteemed worthy of exportation.

In the records left by the Dutch in Ceylon mention is made of the Pearl fisheries having been held by the Kandian Monarchs on banks off Chilaw, and that they occasioned misunderstanding between the Dutch Governors and those Princes. But the Chilaw banks have not been productive for many years.

The valuable fisheries on the banks lying off Aripo, and the beauty of the pearl obtained from them, would seem to indicate some peculiar property in the bottom of that part of the sea. It is well known that the flavour of edible fish depends very much on the nature of the banks over which they are caught; and that those which roam in the unfathomable parts of the ocean are seldom worthy of the sauce required to render them palatable.

To the north-eastward of the Aripo pearl banks there are some extensive reefs of madrepore, some parts of which appear above the surface of the water when it is low; and when the sea is calm and the water clear these coral formations have a most beautiful appearance, some assuming the form of flowers of very large dimensions; but the outer parts being very fragile, it is seldom that they can be removed without injury. The sponges and broken pieces of coral brought up by the divers from the pearl banks abound with varieties of small crabs, worms, and numerous other minute animals, most amusing to the ordinary observer and highly interesting to the naturalist. In some places the sponges are of a cup or tulip shape, and of a bright orange red colour; but their beauty of colour soon fades when they are kept dry.

The mussels called "Pinna," and by the natives "Arkoe," are found in large beds, with the points of their closed fan-like shells sticking two or three inches into the sand. These pinna have been found nearly covered with pearl oysters which have been fished up from off them. There is also a great variety of shell fish, and among them a large conch, called the elephant chank, which feeds on the oysters. The sea over the banks abounds in edible and other fishes, some of which also devour the oysters. I have seen ten pearls and some crushed oyster-shells taken from the stomach of one which is called by the Tamils the "Cl.artee." * Sharks of the ordinary description are frequently seen; and on two occasions my attention has been called to spotted ones of such monstrous size as to make the common ones at their sides appear like pilot fish. Sea snakes are very common, and sometimes land serpents and iguanas venture to swim from the shore. The attention of a seaman on board the *Wellington* was once suddenly attracted to a cobra de capello, by the cold chill caused by its skin coming in contact with his bare foot. This venomous snake had swam off from the land, and had crept up the cable of the vessel while at anchor about a quarter of a mile from the shore.

---

* A drawing of which may be seen in Sir James Emerson Tennent's Work, vol. i., p. 207.

The island of Cardieu lies about five miles to the westward
of Koodremalle, and forms the western side of the harbour
which afforded shelter to the Roman tribute ship in the days
of Claudius.* From the northern end of this island a narrow
sandy ridge, with shallow water on it, extends nearly to the
Aripo Pearl banks. The natives of this part of Ceylon have
a tradition that an Amazon princess, who resided near Kood-
remallé, had the dead from her city buried on an island which
has since disappeared, and of which they believe this sandy
ridge to be the remains ; but I believe it to be a portion of the
strata on which the Isle of Cardieu rests : and in all probability it is sandstone, like that found at Paumben and Adam's
Bridge, also at places on the western coast of Ceylon as far
south as Colombo.

The boats employed at Pearl fisheries are from six to ten
tons burden. Many of them are used in the coasting trade
when and where the monsoon is favourable for such small
craft ; some are common fishing boats, while others are the
licensed boats used for conveying merchandize to and from
shipping in such ports as Colombo ; and when a pearl fishery
is to take place, such as can be spared from their ordinary
work are fitted out for the occasion, and the boatmen proceed
in them with similar feelings to those which animate English
watermen when proceeding to regattas. As these boats have
no projecting keels they do not succeed in sailing very " close
to the wind ;" and therefore when the wind becomes contrary,
or they are overtaken by calm, they depend on their paddles
or oars. With favourable wind they sail well, and have a
beautiful appearance when returning from the fishing ground
with a bright sun shining on their white sails.

Each boat is manned by a crew consisting of a Tindal, or
master ; a Sambarnotee, or representative of the boat-owner ;
a Today, or water baler ; ten divers, and ten Munducks, or
rowers, who also attend on the divers when they are in the

---

* See Sir James Emerson Tennent, vol. i., p. 532.

sea, and pull them and the oysters they have collected up from
the bottom. A Government Peon is generally sent in each
boat to prevent the boatmen helping themselves to pearls, as
three-fourths of the oysters belong to the Government as its
share in the fishery.

The number of boats employed varies from 50 to 300, according to the extent of the bank and the quantity of oysters
estimated to be upon it. They are assembled by advertise-
ment from the coast of Hindostan, as well as Ceylon. When
more arrive than are required, the Tindals of all that are properly equipped draw lots for employment. .In olden times the
duty of inspecting and licensing the boats devolved on the
Master Attendant, and he was remunerated by a fixed fee on
each licence ; but when this fee became collected as revenue to
the State, the reward of the Master Attendant became restricted to the privilege of collecting ten oysters daily from
each fishing boat, in common with the Commandant of the
troops and other persons specially employed at the fisheries ;
but this objectionable mode of remunerating Government
employés was replaced in 1835 by an equivalent allowance from
the Treasury.

The general assemblage at the fishery takes place about
two miles to the southward of the "Doric," * at a very small
village called Silawatorre, which is the Tamil name of a fish
market. The country around it is desert and waste ; the soil
is poor, and the district is subject to lengthened drought ; but
its neighbourhood abounds with wild animals, from peafowls
to elephants, affording ample amusement to sportsmen. At
break of day, in the dry season of the year, the wild beasts of
the forests and the birds of the air may be seen slowly and
peaceably wending their way in search of water in the hollow
places in the bed of the Aripo river.

---

* A building near Aripo, so called from the style of its architecture,
and intended for the double purpose of being seen from the Pearl banks,
and as a secure residence for the Governor in those early days when the
Kandians were our enemies and given to plunder.

Since 1834, some permanent buildings have been erected for conducting the business of the fishery, and for the accommodation of the soldiers employed for the protection of property; but previously the only accommodation afforded for such purposes consisted of temporary huts hastily built with sticks, mats, and leaves. In the short space of a few weeks, this barren plain and sandy shore, of which the sea turtle was previously in peaceful possession, are covered with huts and stalls for the sale of Indian wares and English manufactures to thousands of persons of both sexes assembled from remote places, in all varieties of costume, presenting a peculiarly picturesque appearance and a most exciting scene.

The fisheries are held in March, as soon as the north-east monsoon moderates into land and sea breezes, attended with intervals of calm. But samples of the oysters have previously been taken up, and the particulars respecting the quantity, and estimated value of the pearls found in 1,000 oysters, have been notified to the public.

When the fishing ground has been marked off with buoys bearing flags, and the weather is propitious, a signal gun is fired about midnight for the boats to leave the shore and sail for the banks, to which they are led by the Adapanaars or headmen of the fishery. The chief of these Tamil officers carries a light at the mast-head of his boat as a guide to the fishermen; and he shapes his course for the Government guard-vessel at anchor near to the fishing ground, on board of which a good light is displayed. If the land wind blows strong, the boats reach their destination before daylight, cast anchor, and wait for sunrise. About half an hour after the sun is up a gun is fired, and the ensign hoisted to the mast-head of the Government vessel as the signal for diving to commence, and the Adapanaars lead the way to the spot to be fished.

The presence of the shark charmer on the banks while the divers are at work is found indispensable. This impostor is paid by Government for his attendance, and there are but

very few divers who do not also fee him in some way, generally by giving him some of their share of oysters; for
whether they be Hindoos, Mahomedans, or Parawa Christians, they all have confidence in his incantations. But it is
the noise and the confusion of the multitude assembled, and
the splashing of the water by the divers plunging into the
sea, that alarm and deter the voracious and cowardly sharks
from attacking the divers at Pearl fisheries. They do not
hesitate to attack individuals when diving alone. One poor
man lost both his arms in Colombo Roads, when diving for
the recovery of some property dropped overboard from a ship
while delivering her cargo. Some years ago the shark
charmer on the Aripo banks was requested to exhibit his
power over the fish by assembling some near to the guard-
vessel, but he declined to do so, saying, that it would be improper to trifle with the mystical charm entrusted to his
family for the purpose of keeping sharks away and not for
collecting them together on the pearl banks. On a subsequent
occasion, when preparations were being made for a fishery, a
shark was seen on the bank, and on the charmer being
blamed for neglecting his duty, he promptly declared that as
his power over the fish had been doubted by the gentleman,
he had permitted this one to appear to prove his influence
over it.

Previous to the divers commencing their morning's work,
many of them are seen to be engaged, for a brief interval, in
serious meditation or acts of devotion. They then divest
themselves of their clothes, except a very small piece as a
semblance of decency, and five from each boat plunge into
the sea and swim to their respective sinking stones, which the
boatmen—or, as they are called, munducks, when attending
on the divers—have previously hung over the sides of their
boats in readiness, three stones on one side and two on the
other. Each sinking stone is suspended by a *double* rope,
while the net into which the diver collects the oysters is slung
to a *single* one, in order that he may not mistake one rope for

the other when he is under water. The bight, or double part, of the double cord to which the sinking stone is suspended, is thrown over a stick projecting from the side of the boat within convenient reach of the diver while he is at the surface of the water, for the purpose of enabling him to adjust the height of the stone by lowering or raising it for his foot to rest upon. Before going down he places his right foot upon the stone, and receives its double cord between his toes. He then places his left foot on the lower rim of the hoop to which the net is laced, and presses both hoop and net between his legs, so as to lessen the resistance of the water as he descends. When thus prepared, and assured by the attendant munducks that the cords are clear for being thrown into the sea as he descends, he draws a full breath, presses his nostrils between the thumb and forefinger of his left hand, raises his body to give force to his descent, slips his hold of the bight of the double cord, which instantly flies from over the projecting stick, and descends as rapidly as the stone will sink him to the bottom. On reaching the ground he instantly abandons the sinking-stone, and it is hauled up by his munducks and suspended to the projecting stick in readiness for his next descent. In order to collect the oysters he appears to throw himself on his face and cling to the ground. Some stout men require to have weights in belts round their bodies to enable them to remain at the bottom and creep over considerable space, which, when the oysters are thinly scattered, is sometimes necessary to the extent of eight or ten fathoms. When the diver wishes to ascend, he jerks the cord of the net, which, being held by his watchful attendants in the boat, is instantly felt by them, and they immediately commence hauling up the net as fast as they are able. When the diver has strayed from the spot immediately under the boat for the purpose of collecting the oysters into his net, he has to take care that they do not fall out of it while it is trailing on the bottom of the sea until it becomes directly under the boat; he, therefore, waits until the net is clear of the ground, and so on to boat-

self up its cord hand over hand, his impetus upwards being
accelerated by the net as it is rapidly hauled up by his attendants, he is soon enabled to forsake its cord and bound head
and shoulders out of the water. On reaching the surface he
swims to his sinking stone, and by the time the net is emptied
of its contents, and his attendants are ready, he is prepared to
dive again. This work is repeated by five divers until they
are relieved by the other five who have remained in the boat,
in order to form the necessary alternate rests during the day's
work. From this it will be seen that there are two divers to
each stone, and that one of the two is constantly diving during
the six hours allowed for fishing. When at their regular
work they seldom remain under water more than a minute—
the more usual time being from fifty-three to fifty-seven
seconds—but when requested or paid to remain under water
as long as they are able, I have known them to be immersed
from eighty-four to eighty-seven seconds. They are warned
of the time to ascend by a singing noise in their ears and by
a sensation similar to hiccough. Sometimes they bleed slightly
at the nose and at the ears, but not sufficiently to injure them.
When oysters are plentiful, a diver can collect from three to
four thousand for his day's work. So strong is the desire of
most divers to take up great quantities of oysters that they
are too often regardless of their quality, and it is found extremely difficult to restrain them within the prescribed limits
of the fishing ground, when near to its margin there are
younger oysters to be obtained in larger quantities. This
primitive mode of diving for pearl oysters is not likely to be
superseded by the diving bell or the diving dress. These
modern inventions have been used on the Ceylon Pearl banks
—the former as early as 1826, and the latter in 1836—for the
purpose of ascertaining the nature and condition of the oyster
beds ; but for the practical purpose of collecting oysters it is
evident that one native diver, with his sinking stone and net,
would collect and send up more oysters in a day than all the
men that could be employed in a diving bell, while all the

oysters they could collect would not pay the cost of the labour of English divers.

The weather best suited for pearl fishing is when the land wind dies away soon after sunrise, and the succeeding calm is followed by a sea breeze soon after noon. During the hours of diving the work is kept up with great spirit and eagerness by all parties interested or engaged in the fishery, and the scene is one which affords much pleasure to visitors. But as the continual plunging of so many divers disturbs the water, it is seldom that they can be seen at the bottom. For this purpose it is better to visit the banks during the preparatory inspection, when there are seldom more than twenty divers employed, and their operations may then generally be seen during the period of their immersion. Their nets are often found to contain much that is interesting to those who take pleasure in investigating the wonderful works of the Creator in the recesses of the sea.

When the time approaches for diving to cease for the day the ensign is lowered from the mast-head of the guard-vessel, and the murmuring of thousands of voices is instantly broken by a general call for renewed exertion for the short interval before the work is stopped. At this preparatory signal, the Adapanaars' boats move off the fishing ground, and the Government boats prepare to enforce obedience to the succeeding signal for sailing to the shore. After the ensign has been lowered from fifteen to thirty minutes, according to the success of the divers and the prospect of a continuous sea breeze, a gun is fired as a signal for diving to cease, and for the boats to make sail for the land, when instantly the multitude of divers and boatmen burst forth in louder and more continuous clamour. Some boats' crews who have been fortunate are anxious to push off for the shore, and commence hoisting their sails without delay; while others who are not contented with their loads continue fishing until driven from the banks by the Government boats' crews, and not unfrequently subject themselves to punishment for their obduracy. When all the boats are under weigh and steering for the shore on one of those lovely days so common in March, the delicate whiteness of their primitively formed sails has a peculiarly pleasing effect, and the scene is so beautiful that it never fails to call forth the admiration of all who witness it. As they approach the shore they are welcomed by thousands of persons anxious to learn the success that has attended their adventure. The boats are taken near to their respective cottoos, or spaces fenced off near to the sea shore, and the oysters are conveyed without delay from the boats to within these enclosures, where the contents of each boat is divided by its crew into four heaps as nearly equal as possible. The Government officer, or the renter, if there be one, then selects three heaps, and the fourth is removed by the fishermen as their remuneration, and it is divided by them and the owner of the boat according to their respective shares.

Sometimes the sea breeze is not sufficiently strong to run the boats to the shore before they are overtaken by calm or met by a land wind. In the former case, the boatmen lower their sails, and take to their oars, or paddles, and merrily ply them to their cheerful choruses; and in the latter instance, if the land wind be too fresh to row against, they keep up their sails, and endeavour to reach the shore as near to the fish-market as they can. Sometimes they are carried several miles to leeward before they reach the shore, and then they track their boats with a tow-line along the strand. Although this tedious operation is very fatiguing after their hard work on the banks, they persevere cheerfully until they reach their respective cottoos. When this detention happens to many of the boats, the fishing is suspended for a day in order to refresh the crews; and when the fishing is continued for many days without any other intermission than Sundays, it is sometimes necessary to give the people a day's rest; but when the fishery continues late into April, its operations on the banks are liable to be suspended for several days by strong S.W. winds and high sea, which sometimes continues so long as to put an end to the fishery for the season.

Soon after the fishery has commenced the air at Siláwatorre

becomes tainted with the effluvia from the oysters stored in the cottoos, and the flies rapidly increase and become troublesome. But with the clear weather which generally prevails the power of the sun is so great that the most offensive matter is quickly dried up, and it is astonishing how soon the most sensitive nose becomes accustomed to the smell. Indeed some young gentlemen have declared that it increased their appetite. But if much rain falls the stench becomes intolerable, and it is then that sickness prevails. At the fishery of 1829, the cholera morbus broke out among the poorest parawa coolies, and from them it spread to the several other native classes until it reached the most wealthy, and then the panic became so general that many died on the road while fleeing from the awful scene at Siláwatorre, and the fishery was thus brought to a close before the oysters were all taken from the prescribed bed.

In March of the following year, the oysters which had been left on the bank were taken up, and their pearl proved to be greatly increased in size, and, consequently, in value; so much so, that it was believed the revenue gained at least fifteen thousand pounds by the forced postponement of the previous fishery. This circumstance dispelled the erroneous belief previously entertained that pearl oysters would not survive being disturbed by partial fishing. It also led to the fisheries being more rigidly confined to mature oysters, in order to benefit by the greatest increase in the size and value of their pearl; and notwithstanding some beds have been lost by too long delay, still the revenue has been benefited.

It is not until fishing has ceased for the season, that the washing of the oysters and the collection of their pearl becomes general; but from the commencement of the fishery, the speculators with small means, and others whose necessities or curiosity do not admit of delay, wash their oysters and seek out the pearl at a great loss while the fish is too fresh for the small pearl to be distinguished. The general process of washing the oysters and collecting the pearl is conducted in a very

careful manner. The putrid oysters are put into ballams—
which are canoes, each made of one piece of timber from
twenty to thirty feet long—and sea water is poured upon them
until the ballams are about three-fourths filled, when as many
men as can conveniently arrange themselves on each side
squat down, and wash and examine every shell. Those shells
which have pearls adhering to them are set apart for the
pearls to be cut off, and those free from pearl are cast into
heaps outside the cottoos. The filthy water is then carefully
baled out, and more sea water poured in, until by this continued process nothing appears to be left in the ballams but
sand and pearls. The whole of these remains is then spread
upon white cloth, and exposed to the sun. When thoroughly
dry, women are employed to sift it and collect the pearls, and
when they have finished, it is subjected to the keener scrutiny
of children, whose young eyes detect the smallest seed pearl.
The whole process is vigilantly superintended, and as the
pearl is collected, it is deposited in safety by the superinten-
dent. Dishonest coolies have been known to swallow pearls
in haste in order to avoid detection, and women to conceal
them in their clothes and in their hair.

After all the pearls are collected they are sized, classed,
weighed, and valued. The method of ascertaining their size
is by passing them through a succession of brass colanders.
The colander intended to retain the largest pearls has twenty
perforated holes, all of the same size ; and the pearls that do
not pass through them, after being well shaken, are called of
the 20th basket. The succeeding colander has 30 holes of a
lesser size ; and others, in succession, have 50, 80, 100, 200,
400, 600, 800, and 1,000 holes. Those pearls which pass
through the last colander are called "masie ;" and, being too
small to string, are said to be made into delicate paste for the
wealthy natives to masticate with their betel leaves and areca
nuts, as some men use tobacco. When the pearls have all
been sized by passing through the colanders, each size is
carefully divided into classes according to shape and colour,

and each class is weighed and valued according to its quality.*

Although the demand for pearls in Europe has declined, they continue to be much prized in the East; and after a Ceylon fishery the produce is very soon disposed of for the China and other eastern markets.

It will be seen that the pearl oysters of the Gulf of Manaar are not fished up at all seasons, nor whenever it may please the divers to fish them, as is the case with those larger pearl oysters found in the Persian Gulf and some other places,—the thick shells of which are so valuable for manufacturing purposes in Europe. The success of the Ceylon Pearl fisheries has hitherto depended on a combination of causes in many respects peculiar to the Gulf of Manaar, and not always within human control. In all probability such will continue to be the case, notwithstanding the increasing knowledge of the habits and structure of the fish. But by vigilant attention to the working of Nature, and by not fishing up the oysters before they have attained to maturity, nor by suffering them to remain on the banks until their pearl is lost, considerable casual revenue will no doubt be obtained.

---

* The process by which they are valued is explained in detail in " Steuart's Account of the Pearl Fisheries," printed at Colombo in 1843.

THOSE persons who are engaged in the study of Natural History would do well to possess themselves of Dr. Kelaart's scientific Report on the habits and anatomy of the pearl oyster; from which I venture to extract a few particulars, which I believe should not be passed over unnoticed by me. On the first page of his Report Dr. Kelaart writes :—" Without glass aquaria and a powerful microscope, I should not, perhaps, have obtained even that information on the minute anatomy and habits of the pearl oyster, embodied in this Introductory Report." He then proceeds to enumerate the several articles supplied, and the facilities afforded him for prosecuting his studies on the quiet shore of the inner harbour of Trincomalie, and closes the paragraph with the following words :—" So that no naturalist has, perhaps, ever had the same opportunities of observing the habits of the pearly Mollusc as I have at present." In the fourth paragraph he mentions, that " the Pearl Mollusc resembles more the mussel tribe than the oyster; more particularly as it has, like the mussel, a byssus, or cable, by which it attaches itself to foreign substances, or to others of its kind. The only source of information that I know of on this subject, available to the Ceylon student, is to be found in ' Lebeck's Account of the Pearl Fishery of Ceylon, 1797 ;' to be seen in the Appendix to Captain Steuart's book. The description Mr. Lebeck gives is very imperfect, and excites a smile in the modern naturalist; but this imperfection is excusable in any account written in the infancy of the science of Conchology, and when the microscope was scarcely ever applied to anatomical studies of shells,—at least not in Ceylon." At page 5, he treats on the extreme sensitiveness of the oyster in the following words :—" The tentacles are exceedingly sensitive, and one would almost give them the power of seeing; for not only the touch of a feather, but the approach of one, when the animal is lively and in good health, makes them draw forwards and perfectly shut out the intruder. As these molluscs have no organ of sight, I have no doubt that the delicate nerves which are distributed through the mantle and its tentacular processes, possess in some degree the sense answering to vision in other animals, as well as of touch; for an oyster will be observed rapidly to close its valves on the approach of a hand, or the shadow of a person, near the glass sides of a vessel in which it is confined. I should not, in a popular Report, advert to this physiological subject, but that the senses of the oyster have a great deal to do with its habits, not only in the aquarium, but also in its native bed." Referring to the locomotive power of the oyster, the Doctor observes, that " not the least important part of the animal is the foot. This important member, which has so many useful services to perform in acephalous molluscs, requires a more than ordinary consideration. It is that long, brown, leech-like member, which is seen when the animal is at rest, coiled up in a corner on the right side, above the byssus, which, when protruding out of the shell, and moving about, gives one the popular idea of a tongue.* It is of a dark brown colour above, and whitish beneath; in middle age it is speckled. It is composed of longitudinal and transverse muscular fibres, the latter interlacing between the former, which proceed in two columnar masses from each side of the adductor muscle; between the bundles of fibres are placed the abdominal viscera. From its base is sent off, posteriorly, a glistening white fibrous band; this is attached to the duplicature of the mantle, near the angle of the valves. Thus the foot is seen to be admirably adapted for locomotive powers; and also serves, by its connection with the adductor muscle, to lengthen or shorten the cable or byssus. The foot, in a full-

---

* So called by Lebeck.

sized oyster, is about two and a-half inches long when extended; at rest, it is not more than one and a-half inch in
length. It is broad at the base, tapering to a conical point;
the upper surface is rounded and smooth, the lower flattened
and grooved. The groove extending from the base, terminates
at the point in an oval cup-like fosset. This groove is lined
by a secreting membrane, and is an exact mould for the formation of the byssus, at the will of the animal. When it finds
a necessity for making one, the foot is protruded out of the
shell, and with the tip it seeks out a spot where it can rest the
terminal disc of the groove. If not satisfied with the substance
or position of the stone, or any other matter on which it rests,
it removes to another more suitable spot; for a few minutes
(say five or six if the animal is strong) it rests, and is then
retracted within the shell, leaving behind a strong fibre with
an oval disc, of the form of the groove in the foot. This
whitish fibre is attached to the base of the foot at one end,
and to the rock, or to the shell of another oyster, at the other.
In a day or two this fibre becomes of a bronzed greenish
colour, and looks like hair, with a broad flattened oval root
attached to the rock. This process is again and again repeated, at intervals of a few minutes, till a sufficiently strong
cable is formed. In a large oyster, removed from the sea,
upwards of fifty such fibres form a thick, strong cable, or
byssus, which is attached to the base of the foot by a bifur-
cated fleshy root. The animal cannot detach the byssus from
the rock to which it is attached ; but it has the power of casting it off its own body and leaving it behind, (like a ship
letting slip her cable and anchor in a storm, and sailing off to
sea,) in order to make another byssus, either on the same rock
or on any other convenient place.

" I observed all this process in the aquarium, at a very
early period of my investigations; and was not surprised to
find that the pearl oyster, having nearly the same organs as
the mussel, should form and reform its byssus. But I was
agreeably satisfied in learning, by these observations, that

Captain Steuart, in his valuable and interesting Monograph on the Pearl Fisheries of Ceylon, was incorrect in denying to the pearl oyster this faculty. He states that '*it is not held that pearl oysters have the power to detach themselves, or to re* *at their own will.*' I have not only satisfied myself, and many friends who have seen the oysters in the aquaria which I have established, that the pearl oyster can detach or unmoor itself, but likewise that it walks away with its foot foremost and the shell behind; and does not, as Captain Steuart observes, '*move with its hinges in advance.*' This shuffling movement alone attracted Captain Steuart's attention, but it is an unimportant one, as all bivalves without a byssus have it; and it is independent of the will of the animal, owing to the valves being opened and closed for the purpose of respiration. How imperfect must Captain Steuart—a candid inquirer—now say, have been his long observations, when the oyster is seen, night after night, taking a walk round the inside of a chatty, or mounting the glass side of a vivarium, forming here and there a byssus. It is most unfortunate that he and others should not have made these observations, which are so simple in their nature, but yet conclusive of the possibility '*of trans-* *lating pearl oysters from their original rocky beds to their more* *convenient locations.*' "

If Dr. Kelaart had remembered, that, although he was " present at two of the largest Pearl fisheries ever made off Aripo in 1835 and 1836," * he failed to make the discovery alluded to, he probably would not have made this reflection on the imperfect observation of one who is not a Naturalist, and whose time was too fully occupied with the active concerns of the fishery to admit of his paying watchful attention to the movements of the pearl oyster, even had he been supplied with an aquarium and other instruments and materials for the purpose. In order that the Doctor should no longer be under

---

* See page 18 of his Report.

misapprehension as to the nature of my connexion with the
Pearl fisheries, immediately on the receipt of his Report I
wrote to him, and referred him to the copy of Mr. Deputy
Secretary Lusignan's letter in the Appendix to my "Account
of the Fisheries," which he had in his possession. In this
official letter, dated the 1st June, 1822, addressed to the Collector of Manaar, conferring on that officer " the additional
office of Supervisor of the Pearl Banks, with an additional
salary for that duty of £300 per annum," the official duty of
the Master Attendant in relation to the Pearl Banks is set
forth in the following words:—" The inspection of March
will of course be the most complete, because the period in
which examinations can be conducted is the longest; and the
Master Attendant of Colombo will on these occasions be sent
down to lay down, by nautical survey, the projections in which
your inspection is made, and to which your joint Report will
allude."

It is true, that in relation to the Pearl fisheries, the Master
Attendant was sometimes designated Inspector of the Pearl
Banks; but in my official appointment, in the *Gazette* an-
nouncing it to the public, and in the warrant I held for the
protection of the banks, there is no mention whatever of such
office. In *all* I am designated Master Attendant. But, in fact,
the duty as laid down in Mr. Secretary Lusignan's letter is
purely a professional one, and, as such, included in those relating to marine surveys, shipping, and navigation, for which
the Master Attendant is responsible to the Government. But
although there was no salary allowed to the Inspector of Pearl
Banks, there were privileges allowed the officers who were
temporarily employed at Pearl fisheries, which consisted of a
certain number of oysters collected daily from each fishing-
boat on its return from the banks; and, as one of these officers, the Inspector of Pearl Banks was entitled to receive ten.
After I discovered that the collection of these oysters by native *employés* was attended by unwarrantable exactions, op-
pressive to the fishermen, I recommended that all these

privileges should be commuted for their equivalent in money, and paid to each officer by the Government.* In 1835 this arrangement was adopted, and the fishermen were relieved of the imposition.

Soon after the Pearl fishery in 1835, a Naval Supervisor was appointed to reside at Aripo, in special charge of the Pearl banks, on a salary of £500 a year, and the Collector of Manaar ceased to draw the salary of £300 ; while I, having no salary in connexion with the Pearl banks, became relieved of an unpleasant duty, and as I ceased to attend the Pearl fishery, I also ceased to claim the commuted allowance before alluded to.

Some time after the Pearl banks ceased to be productive, the Naval Supervisor resigned the appointment, and, in the absence of a successor, the duty being on the sea, devolved on the Master Attendant. As I had done the work before 1836, so I resumed it,—the difference being, that in the former instance while I did the duty, the Collector of Manaar enjoyed the salary of Supervisor ; and in the latter case, while I did the work, the Government saved the payment of the salary.

After a long interval of disappointment and much fruitless search, I at length perceived the prospect of a coming series of fisheries on the Aripo banks, and I remained in Ceylon, contrary to medical advice, to be present at its commencement, so that in case of failure I might be certain of its cause. The successful series commenced in March, 1855, and I left Ceylon in June of the same year.

As I never professed to be a close observer of the works of Nature, I might have passed over unheeded Dr. Kelaart's allusion to my " imperfect observation" of such matters, but he is not the only person who has misapprehended my connexion with the Pearl fisheries. I stated in my original account of the Pearl fisheries, that my official connexion with

---

* See page 62 in my Colombo Account of the Fisheries.

them was purely professional, as Master Attendant; that the Collector of the District of Manaar, off which the Pearl banks lie, was their salaried Supervisor when I entered the Ceylon public service; that promotion in the Civil Service occasioned five different gentlemen to hold the office within the short space of three years; that the Commissioners of Inquiry considered that the Master Attendant's duties at Colombo did not admit of his passing sufficient time on the Pearl banks, and that their necessary supervision could not be expected of Supervisors unaccustomed to the sea, and so frequently changed, and that, under these impressions, they recommended the appointment of a Naval Supervisor to reside permanently at Aripo. I also stated that, on the resignation of the Naval officer so appointed, the work of his office, and not his salary, devolved upon me as Master Attendant. Notwithstanding my statement of all these particulars in 1843, I have since seen it reported to the Secretary of State, that " the Master Attendant's duty in relation to the Pearl fisheries had, through the failure of that source of revenue, become nearly a sinecure;" and after the successful Pearl fishery in 1855, the money allowance fixed in 1835, in lieu of the ten oysters collected daily from each fishing boat, was refused me as being an obsolete custom. In one case I was deprived of the commuted allowance for a privilege abolished on my own recommendation; and in the other I was represented as almost a sinecurist, while performing really hard work without payment.